WHACKY
Toys, Whirligigs & Whatchamacallits

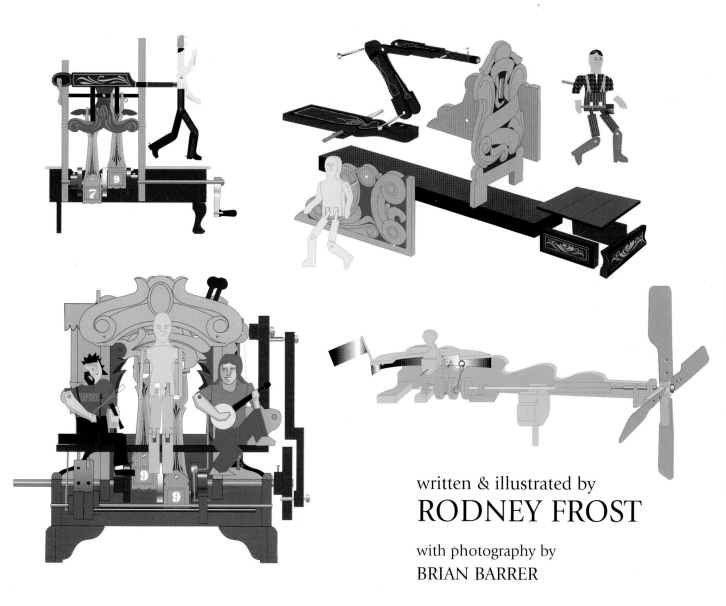

written & illustrated by
RODNEY FROST

with photography by
BRIAN BARRER

Sterling Publishing Co., Inc.
New York

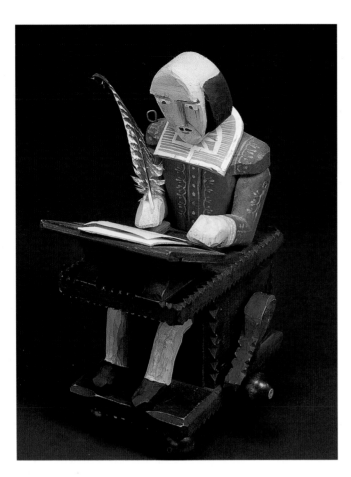

People often ask me whether the toy that I am showing them is a reproduction or replica. One time a lady asked how old was the toy I was busking with and it was almost like the joke of the worker asked about how much experience he has and he looks at his watch.

The piece that I was trying to make money with that day I had finished the night before! It's not that I try to make them look old—I try to make them look fresh and clean and new—it's just that I like to make things interesting. I reach right into the cluttered corners of my brain and enjoy finding stuff. Then I put them together; often I surprise myself with what I find. When I bring things out, they have traces of other things on them. Maybe some cherubs have got squished against an elephant for a number of years. Imagine that! Let's see if that will work, make me think of something else or just get left on the shelf to await the suggestions of spiders.

Here is a toy that I'm *not* going to draw out for you completely, but once you do a few of the ones I do draw, you can not only draw it yourself, you can make it. See if you can figure out how the hand and head of "The Writer" might move. Once you've had a go at designing your own mechanism, take a look at the back of the book and you will see some hints in the photograph and the drawing of the crank mechanism I came up with.

Library of Congress Cataloging-in-Publication Data
Frost, Rodney.
  Whacky toys, whirligigs & whatchamacallits / Rodney Frost.
    p. cm.
  ISBN 0-8069-9286-7
  1. Wooden toy making. I. Title: Whacky toys, whirligigs and whatchamacallits. II. Title.

TT174.5.W6 F675 2002
745.592--dc21   2002021694

10 9 8 7 6 5 4 3 2 1
Published by Sterling Publishing Co., Inc.
387 Park Avenue South, New York, NY 10016
© 2002 by Rodney Frost
Distributed in Canada by Sterling Publishing
c/o Canadian Manda Group, One Atlantic Avenue, Suite 105
Toronto, Ontario, Canada M6K 3E7
Distributed in Great Britain and Europe by Chrysalis Books
64 Brewery Road, London N7 9NT, England
Distributed in Australia by Capricorn Link (Australia) Pty. Ltd.
P.O. Box 704, Windsor, NSW 2756 Australia
Printed in China
All rights reserved

Sterling ISBN 0-8069-9286-7

Book design: Judy Morgan
Editor and layout design: Rodman Pilgrim Neumann

The text is set in Giovanni Book

What makes me want to make these things I don't know.

Sometimes I'll see something when I was looking through a book—something little in a picture—such as eyebrows, and it looks to me as if they could move up and down by themselves.

I say, "I was looking through a book" because that's how I "read" books—I look at the pictures and then I read what's under them and then if I need still more information I'll look at the words in the text—some scholarly people pooh-pooh this idea of how to get knowledgeable but it works for me and just about anyone else that uses it.

So, anyway I was looking at a book about Northwest Indian art and customs (I read just about everything I can get my hands on. My brain can take it—your brain can take it!) and there was a section on masks. One of the masks had eyebrows that were pieces of tin, tacked on—this got me thinking right away. I scribbled a picture of a face with the eyebrows swinging up and wondered how this could be done, not the whole thing just the eyebrow. Later, I thought, I can figure out how to get the eyebrows connected to the winder.

After the eyebrows the next natural thing to put in is the eyes and I'll think of what the eyes can do—rotate is the obvious choice so draw in the eyes rotating.

Jaws are good for action. Now I am beginning to get some idea of the support system that I will need to construct the toy and what I want it to be. I have-to/can-if-I-want-to bring the support down or away from the items already thought of. I scribble in some possible needed mechanisms. Here I notice the similarities of the parts and their movements, the eyebrows have a rotation movement, the eyes have a rotation, but the jaw will need to move up and down. Generally toys operate best with a rotating handle, so I'm working with rotation—straight pulleys for the eyes and eyebrows—maybe a crank for the jaw to convert to up and down motion.

I keep working down the body looking for other things that can move, draw in the back board, and wonder why I'm doing this thing some more. After I put in the crank to operate it, the whole thing begins to look like something that gives me an idea of what it is about.

At this point I must start making it or it will be a drawing project only. Later I will use pencil and paper to clarify some thoughts or problems to be solved with the mechanism.

Contents

Everything Moves, Propellers & Whirligigs

Making whirligigs is fun. A lot of enjoyment can be got from watching the wind set your creation in frantic motion. But just as much as I enjoy watching the antics, I also love to just look at the prop going around by itself. Sometimes that's just what you need to relax yourself or realize that the old world is still going on outside your window.

I don't know why that is but it's true—you feel a bit down and there out the window is the weather vane popping around or maybe a bird's sitting on it—you feel good again.

My friend, Christine, looked after one of my whirligigs once. She put it by the bird feeder and on days when there was no wind the little birds would sit on the blades and get a ride!

This is not an exact book. The measurements in it are not, sometimes, to be taken too seriously.

Making things is like dealing with people. No one would imagine that if a person were made to go to bed at an exact time they would always wake up at exactly the time planned or if we fed someone an exact amount of food they would grow to an exact size. Oh, we try sometimes and get perplexed sure enough, frustrated might be a better word. Everything is itself, we have to allow the other things to be themselves.

Improvisation is essential when using the various instructions I've given here—if something doesn't quite fit according to the book, adjust it a bit. Wood changes shape and texture when it comes in contact with anything else in this world. Water and dampness swell the fibers and what was working yesterday is now solid and jammed. Then again, what was moving beautifully when you packed up for the night has now dried out and doesn't fit at all. There are a number of solutions to such problems. You will figure those out as they occur. For now the main thing to remember is this—stay calm. Calmness and the feeling that you will solve this problem (and others, because there will be others!) together with time, the age old remedy, will get you through.

Speaking of which—time, I mean—take lots of time, don't rush. On the other hand, making something is kind of like riding a bicycle; you have to get some kind of momentum or you're never really riding! Swimming with one foot on the bottom is not really swimming. Once both feet are off the ground there is nothing quite like it. Buoyed up, balanced, and making no sudden moves, above all not panicking when things seem a little scary, that's what making things is like.

MAKING A PROPELLER FROM WOOD

Take a long stick of wood about the proportion shown here. Drill a hole in the center. A little way from one side of the hole make a saw cut at an angle, as shown. Cut away the wood from the saw cut to the end. Do the same on the other end of the stick.

Turn the stick over and repeat the operation. Put a nail through the hole and attach to some object.

Pitch is the angle that the blade makes to the wind. Different pitches give different efficiencies, like gears. Try some.

When wind (moving air) meets an object, it has to go somewhere—it doesn't just disappear, it bounces off (deflects).

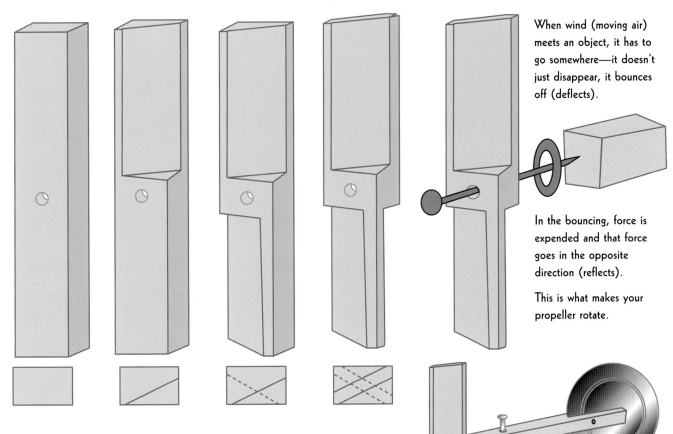

In the bouncing, force is expended and that force goes in the opposite direction (reflects).

This is what makes your propeller rotate.

MAKE A WEATHER-VANE WHIRLIGIG WITH YOUR PROPELLER

Fix the blade to a long stick, add a vane, balance on another stick, attach, and enjoy!

For the vane I've used a coffee tin top set in a saw cut. You might like to try something more sophisticated. (Be careful of the sharp edges of the tin!)

There's a bead on the nail as a bearing. Wooden beads are good to keep around for many uses. This is one of them.

Holding the stick in your fingers—gently blow toward the thing that you have made. You will see that the coffee tin end, the vane, moves away from you and there it stays.

No matter how hard you blow, it will not continue to turn. This is part of the principle of a whirligig. The end that has the largest surface area will turn away from the wind.

The vane will not turn around and around because, when it gets farthest away and starts to move around the pivot, it meets the wind coming from the other side.

You may wonder why these things are called "weather" vanes. The reason is that movement of air over the earth and the interaction of the air with the ground warming and cooling create rain, dry spells, and what we call weather. The direction of the wind can help us determine what kind of weather we can expect.

In order to get stuff out of your brain you have to have stuff in it. Our so called teaching system seems more intent upon keeping you on the straight and narrow and any exploration is confined to what is "found" there. An Easter egg hunt for sure! Ideas and discovery are up to you. Libraries, junk stores, antique auctions, the backs of buildings will give you something to think about—something to remember. Put it in the stock room that is your brain.

I seem to be able to remember stuff from way back before I was even around. Not by any feat of reincarnation but because England was shifted back half a century during the time when I was a kid. When the 1939–45 war was going on, horses had been given a reprieve and all that went with them—carts, wagons, drays, blacksmith shops, horse shit, untarred roads existed as living heritage and memories. Creaking, grinding delivery trucks brought milk and bread on iron-shod wheels and hooves. The little guy down the street with the great furniture moving van—what we called a pantechnicon—a team of Belgian bays who ate their dinner

A METAL-BLADE PROPELLER

Make blades out of any thing that seems suitable. Aluminum siding is a good source of metal for blades. You can use the tops from tin cans for an interesting effect.

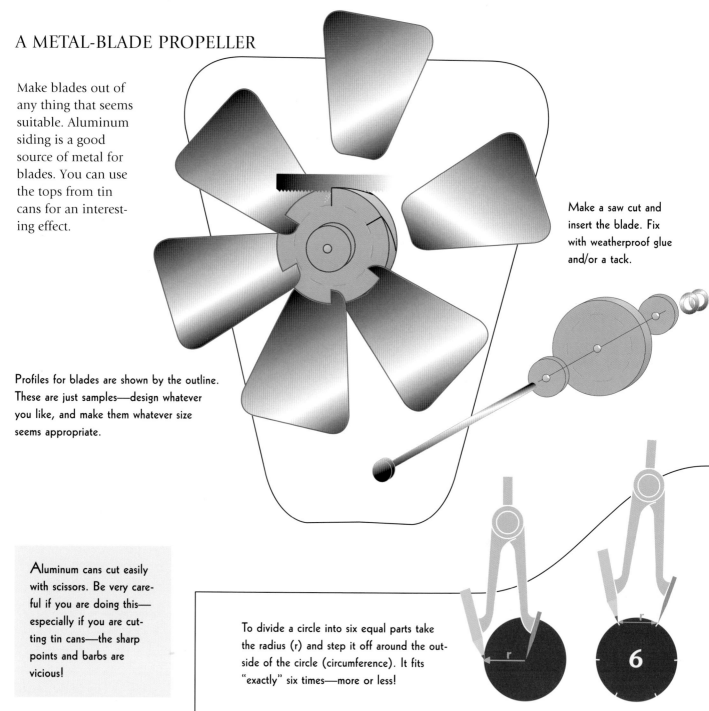

Make a saw cut and insert the blade. Fix with weatherproof glue and/or a tack.

Profiles for blades are shown by the outline. These are just samples—design whatever you like, and make them whatever size seems appropriate.

Aluminum cans cut easily with scissors. Be very careful if you are doing this— especially if you are cutting tin cans—the sharp points and barbs are vicious!

To divide a circle into six equal parts take the radius (r) and step it off around the outside of the circle (circumference). It fits "exactly" six times—more or less!

(lunch) from nose bags at the curb while he ate his indoors behind the lace windows and by the parrot cage. When I got a haircut, the barbershop had stuffed birds and amber colored photos of anxious young men from Southwick, winners of the East Sussex Football Association Championships, fifty years before—in the nineteenth century!

Maybe some of the men in the pictures were the ones who came occasionally to our street. They had a box on a stick. About the size of an apple box and at about waist height. When we saw one coming, we would rush in to get a penny from mum and, when we had all gathered around and given him our money, he would wind or pull back the curtains on the front of the box and start the show. I can't remember many of the shows; in fact, I can only clearly recall little jointed men sawing and hammering in a tiny workshop. Each one doing his task operated by the man who wound the handle at the side. It was worth every penny!

In the late forties my Dad, Alan my brother, and I would go on holiday roving the train routes

MAKING A POWERFUL PROPELLER

Simply constructed and really only a step away from the propeller on the previous page, this propeller can produce a lot of power. The pictures tell all you need to know.

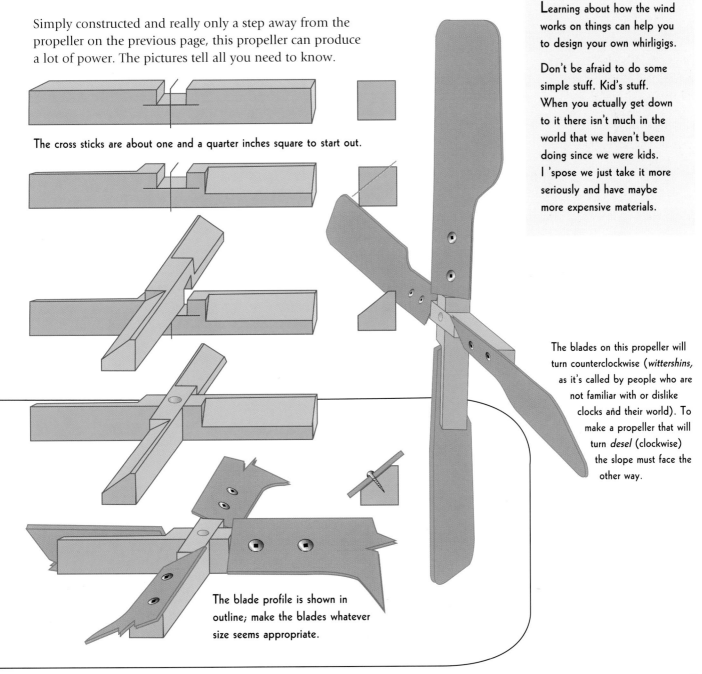

The cross sticks are about one and a quarter inches square to start out.

The blade profile is shown in outline; make the blades whatever size seems appropriate.

Learning about how the wind works on things can help you to design your own whirligigs.

Don't be afraid to do some simple stuff. Kid's stuff. When you actually get down to it there isn't much in the world that we haven't been doing since we were kids. I 'spose we just take it more seriously and have maybe more expensive materials.

The blades on this propeller will turn counterclockwise (*wittershins*, as it's called by people who are not familiar with or dislike clocks and their world). To make a propeller that will turn *desel* (clockwise) the slope must face the other way.

around Sussex. In Eastbourne there was a Lifeboat Museum. In the museum was a big glass case half filled with murky water. To the right a dim coastal town with a lifeboat shed prominent. To the left the great imaginary sea beyond the dusty lighthouse and waiting rocks.

For tuppence (twice the usual rate, so my brother had to be convinced that we both wanted to see it even though we had seen it last year and the year before) the show commenced.

First the waves of the murky sea appeared, choppy and vicious. The lighthouse shone its bright beam out and revolved revealing—Too Late!— a ship is on the rocks (now wet and shiny). The tin maroon on a stick goes up! The lifeboat shed doors click madly open. The lifeboat is launched! Down the brass ramp through the murky whipped up water and to the rocks. Hurrah!

How the next bit was done mechanically I don't remember, but the passengers from the wrecked ship are transferred by breeches buoy to the life boat all the while

WHAT IS A PANTANENOME?

Here is a *pantanenome* (pan-ta-nen-o-mee); the name means "all-winds."

This propeller will turn without having to turn into the wind. This means that one can be free of the traditional weather-vane whirligig shape.

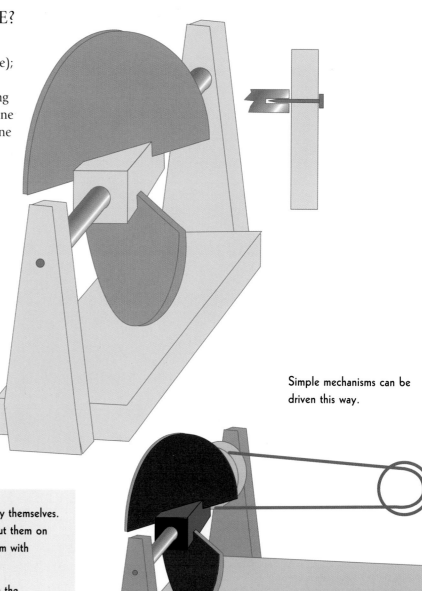

Simple mechanisms can be driven this way.

Pantanenomes are fun to build just by themselves. I once built a number of them and put them on the fence. They really turn! Paint them with patterns, colors, you name it.

Go crazy—they'll have that effect on the squirrels in your area too!

battered by wind and rain and water. On the backdrop tin clouds passed across the view (these were worked on continuous chains like a shooting gallery, even a kid could see that!).

After the lifeboat returned to shore, the water calmed to a flat empty surface. The whirring stopped.

Some time later I started making my own toys.

The world has changed a lot. Digital has deprived us of the whirring, clanking, and puffing. Squeaks and groans that used to tell us of efforts, strains, and troubles have been replaced by eeps and beeps. Worst of all—the blank screen!

I had thought the first machine I showed on the street with its levers, wheels, and moving parts would not be well received by kids who were so used to computer screens and video games. I was wrong.

Little kids in strollers, sophisticated teens, punks, lovers, yuppies all enjoy the toys you wind. You will too!

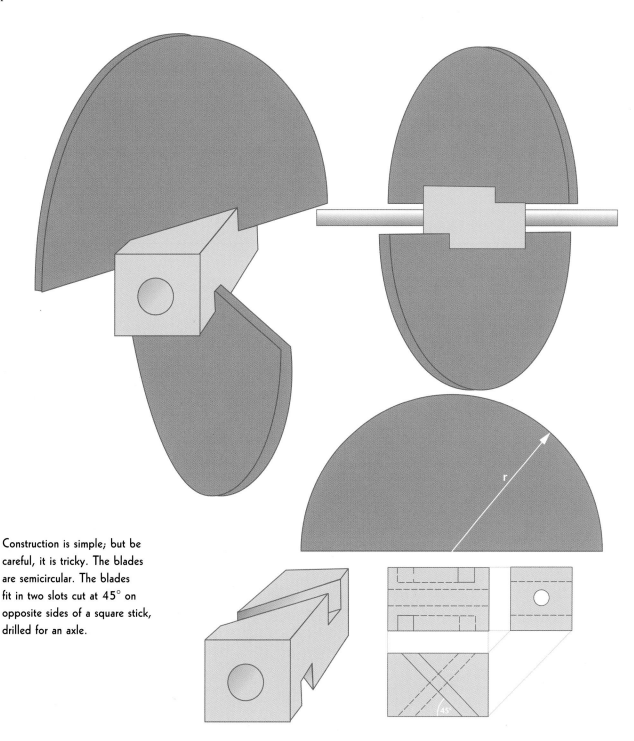

Construction is simple; but be careful, it is tricky. The blades are semicircular. The blades fit in two slots cut at 45° on opposite sides of a square stick, drilled for an axle.

Sunny Days in Limberjack Heaven

*E*verybody's the same and everybody's different. Dolls are like people. If you see a whole lot of them and they are all the same—that's scary. My friend Jeff runs art classes for what I like to call old people of all ages. He starts his classes out by everyone shaking hands with everyone else and saying, "I recognize your differences and I acknowledge the samenesses," and this creates a wonderful nonthreatening atmosphere in which to work.

So when you are making these dolls, don't worry if they look different from what you expected; don't fret if the legs are a bit too long, or the eyes are too close—like we used to say (and still do) what you can't hide, make a feature of.

Did you ever ask someone for a recipe of some really good tasting food? Then, when you used the recipe, it wasn't quite the same thing. This is because, when a person makes something, they use a lot of preferences. These preferences are personal; they come from the way a person lives and feels and acts and what they like and love—and all these things affect what we do. Even when it comes to measuring out flour and whether we pick the biggest egg or the one almost the same size but slightly smaller to put into the mixing bowl. It says one cup; but is that cup full or just a bit short? Same with making toys; sometimes your three-quarters of an inch is not the same as mine. Add up all the differences and the thing comes out different. Just like we are different; you are you—and I am me. Nothing wrong with that; we *are* different.

Since this is our beginning project, I've put in quite a bit of detail that, later on, I'll expect you to know and use your common sense—or whatever you've got. But for now bear with me—some of you know this and some of you don't—differences, right?

Bodies

The body is basically just a slab of wood; but it doesn't have to stay that way. We can make it whatever shape we want it to be. I've given here some shapes that I've found to work, and they will make the Limberjacks that you can see arrayed in the photograph on the opening spread.

Bits & Pieces

This is the plan of a tricorn hat and a snowshoe. You can add whatever you want. Experiment with your own styles and characters.

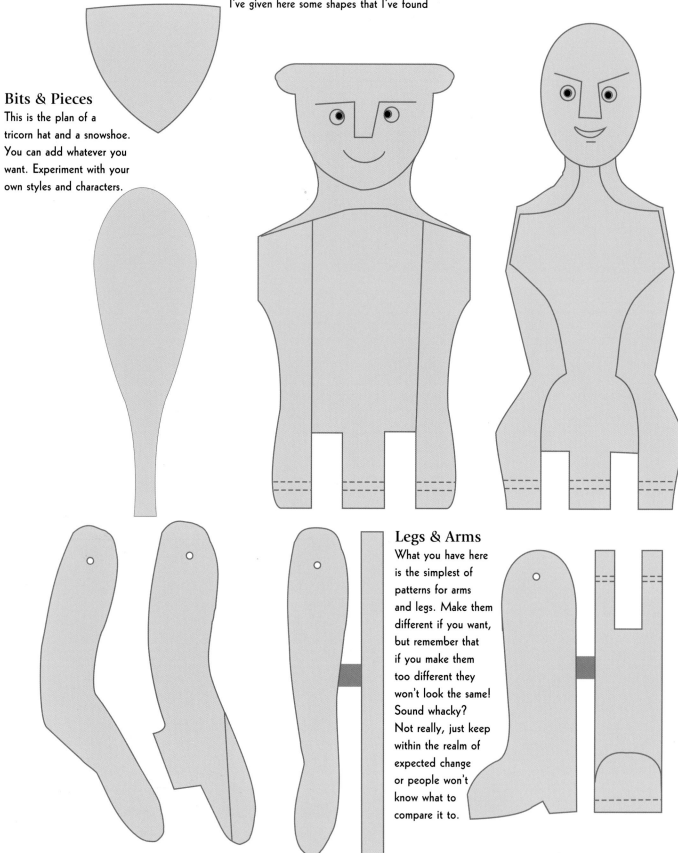

Legs & Arms

What you have here is the simplest of patterns for arms and legs. Make them different if you want, but remember that if you make them too different they won't look the same! Sound whacky? Not really, just keep within the realm of expected change or people won't know what to compare it to.

HOW THE LIMBERJACK DANCES

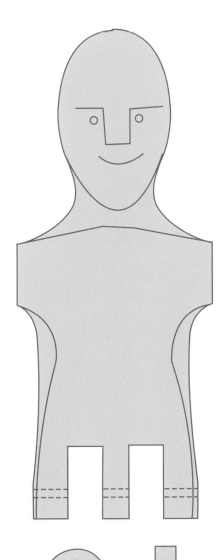

When I first started making and selling these little guys, I had really never made one dance—I'd jiggled one around but I always thought that it took years to learn how to do this fun thing. I was wrong. One day I was at a street fair and I got tired of apologizing and making excuses like "I'm not too good at this, you should see old so-and-so dance these little devils." I realized, of course, that I must have been doing this "fake" dancing with the Limberjack about 30 seconds longer than the person that was thinking of buying it and, anyway, let them have the treat of thinking to themselves, "I could do better than that!" After that brilliant revelation, I got myself a tin sandwich and a harness for my neck to leave my hands free and whoopdi do. We was in business!

Now folks say "Yes that's nice but I can't play the harmonica"! Well—you don't have to because the Limberjack is an instrument—musician friends of mine actually call them instruments. So, here's what to do.

Get a comfortable place to sit—flat and smooth like a kitchen chair or, if you are outside, a low wall is good—and put the paddle under your bum. In other words—sit on the paddle board. Lightly hold the stick in the Limberjack's back and hold him out over the end of the board/paddle so that his feet are just touching.

Listen to the music (yours or someone else's) and tap the paddle in time to the music with your other hand. You don't have to move the stick up and down but by experiment (and accident) you will find that, if you do move the stick a little left–right, the bonhomme will respond with many variations that will be entirely its own. The arms will whirl, the feet will fly, and here's another thing— when you both get to that stage ideas will come to you about dancing and music that will get everyone laughing.

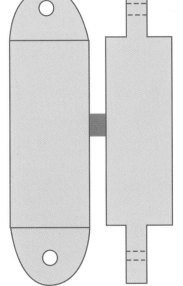

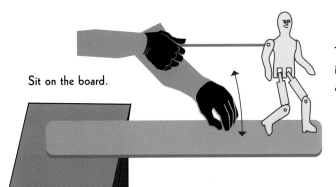

Sit on the board.

Turn to the next page for instructions on how to make a *Bonhomme*—Limberjack.

Limberjacks or as we call them in Canada, *Bonhommes,* have been around for a long time. Find a book on the history of toys and you'll find jointed dolls. I first found them in a book called *Foxfire* that was produced by schoolkids—if you like toys and interesting homemade things look it up in most libraries. Elliot Wigginton was the teacher who organized that wonderful event— Thanks Elliot!

The Body

Trace or photocopy the body, from pages 12 or 13. Use a piece of bristol board if you think that you are going to make more than one—maybe not now but later, sure you are.

Cut it out and place it on a piece of one-inch pine with the longest dimension lined up and running the same way as the grain. Cut the body out. At the bottom where the legs will join cut straight across at B.

Now turn the body upside down (you might like to clamp it in something like a vise for this or clamp it to the edge of a table with a G clamp) and saw down to the line. You can use your saber saw, tenon saw, or coping saw—whatever you've got and are comfortable with.

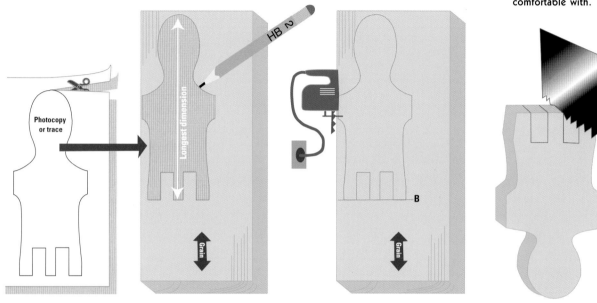

Legs

Trace or photocopy the leg outlines, from pages 12 or 13, and lay them out on a piece of one-inch pine just as you did for the body.

After they are cut out, mark the place for the slot to be on the boot part of the leg. Mark where the tenons are to be cut on the thighs.

Stick

This is a piece of ¼" dowel. Whittle one out of a branch—that's nice too!

Boot Leg Parts

Saw again, just as with the body—try not to go too far down; but anyway, if you do, don't worry, start another leg—more fun for you!

Turn the leg sideways and chop out the slot. You'll probably have to put it on a block with the toe end hanging over.

Thighs

Saw down just like before. Turn it sideways and saw off the cheeks. Be careful.

This is tricky stuff; so don't go getting mad or start calling yourself names, because this is hard work and you need the energy that getting mad takes and you need confidence to finish things up nicely. Trust me.

The Board or Paddle

A piece of thin plywood, such as "door skin" is made of, is ideal. Cut a piece at least 18" long and 4" wide. Sand the edges smooth and round the corners; it comes mighty close to some important body parts!

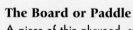

Leg Slots

Place the body on a flat and sturdy surface, such as a bench or a plank on the ground. With a ⅜" chisel hit down on the line as I've show here. Turn it over and then again; after a while that little square bit of wood will come out.

At this point you've got quite a way from a block of wood, and anyone will recognize it as a human shape; but it is nice to whittle away some more to make your Limberjack a bit more gorgeous than plain old Mr. Plankhead!

GETTING IT TOGETHER

With all of the pieces made, it's hardly any time before you will be entertaining.

A common nail is okay for the arm joint; if you want you could use a long thin screw—it's best to be on the safe side.

For the hip and knee joints I use bamboo meat skewers; they are cheap but they are also of inconsistent thickness. So, if one is a bit sloppy for the size of the hole, get another out of the packet until you find a good fit. Hammer them through the holes and snip off the ends with side-cutter pliers; you can cut them off with a knife but it takes patience.

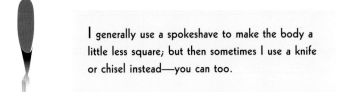

I generally use a spokeshave to make the body a little less square; but then sometimes I use a knife or chisel instead—you can too.

Stick Hole

There is a ¼" hole in his back to take the stick.

Arms

Whittle them to look the way you want.

About Holes

The idea is to have some holes loose and some tight; so the different sizes are detailed here. Before you snip off the dowel, test and wiggle it to make sure the joint moves freely. If it doesn't, then fix it.

Faces

Most of my faces start out the same—just as my bodies start out the same—but they don't end up that way. Here's my face formula.

Lay the body on a flat surface and take a chisel—any size will do but probably a half inch or (in my case, my favorite) ¾". Hit the face part of the body three times, sort of like eyebrows and under the nose. Now gently (use a driver of some kind—a mallet or the side of your hammer) cut up to the nose line. It'll be wider than the nose, but don't mind because next move the chisel a little to the side and cut out the cheeks and up to the eyebrow line.

The side of the nose will need a bit of attention. So just wheedle it out with the chisel turned or use a knife.

Features

Eyes are punched in with a nail set or cut-off nail—something round, pointy, and flat on the end. For the mouth I use a gouge, but I sometimes use a piece of pipe; hit in at a slant for a nice smile! Or you want a miserable one? Turn it upside down.

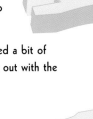

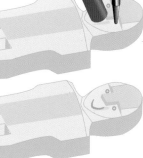

If you want to put a little lubricant on the joints, use some petroleum jelly (Vaseline).

Monsieur Raquette et Two Friends

"You know what would be great," says my son the folk musician who plays one of my Limberjacks as part of his act. "It would be great to have a machine that I could use to dance this little guy (pointing to the Limberjack) and be able to have my hands free to play the bones or washboard at the same time!"

That was enough for me to start thinking and then scribbling my ideas. Some of the ideas didn't work out; too complicated, too complicated!

Finally I had this thing made and—since I had one of the characters wearing snowshoes and the French for snowshoe is raquette and this toy makes such one hell of a noise that you can hardly hear the band anyway— I called it "Monsieur Raquette et Two Friends." That way I can use both of Canada's official languages.

Monsieur Raquette is a foot-operated machine with interchangeable Limberjacks. The starting dancer is the showshoer, and I gave him the company of a lumberjack Limberjack and a voyageur Limberjack who wait at the side for their turns. The Limberjack dances when the foot pedal is depressed and released repeatedly. Very simple!

I had thought when I first started showing these pieces that people's interest would be more attuned to the gizmos we have around us, like the electronic gadgets so many seem to be unable to do without. But there is tremendous enthusiasm for the physically mechanical; the crank toys but also the simple lever-operated toys like this one. These are play things and delights, not really toys as we have come to use the word; machines that surprise and engage the operator, both visually appealing and intriguing to make. Go ahead, have fun! Make one of these wooden wonders.

Schematic Drawings of Basic Construction
of the Toy's Framework

T ake one plank about as long as from the ground up to your hand, thickish and a bit wider than your hand, and use this as a base. (Dimensions for the more modern toymaker shown here.)

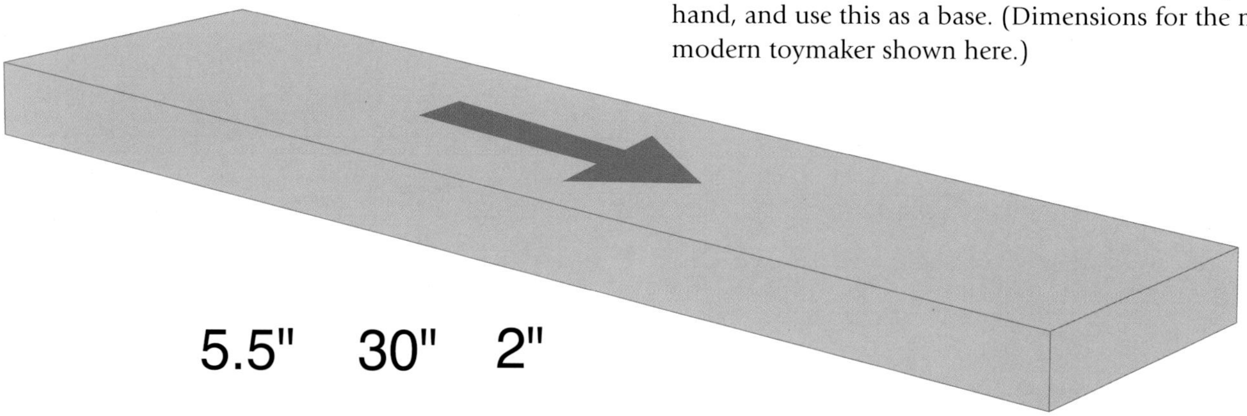

5.5"   30"   2"

Get some planks of what is called "one-by" stock pine (see "Nominal Sizes of Wood" below) or what you like working with (and can afford) at least nine inches wide—or join some pieces together edge to edge. The glue that one can get nowadays is very reliable.

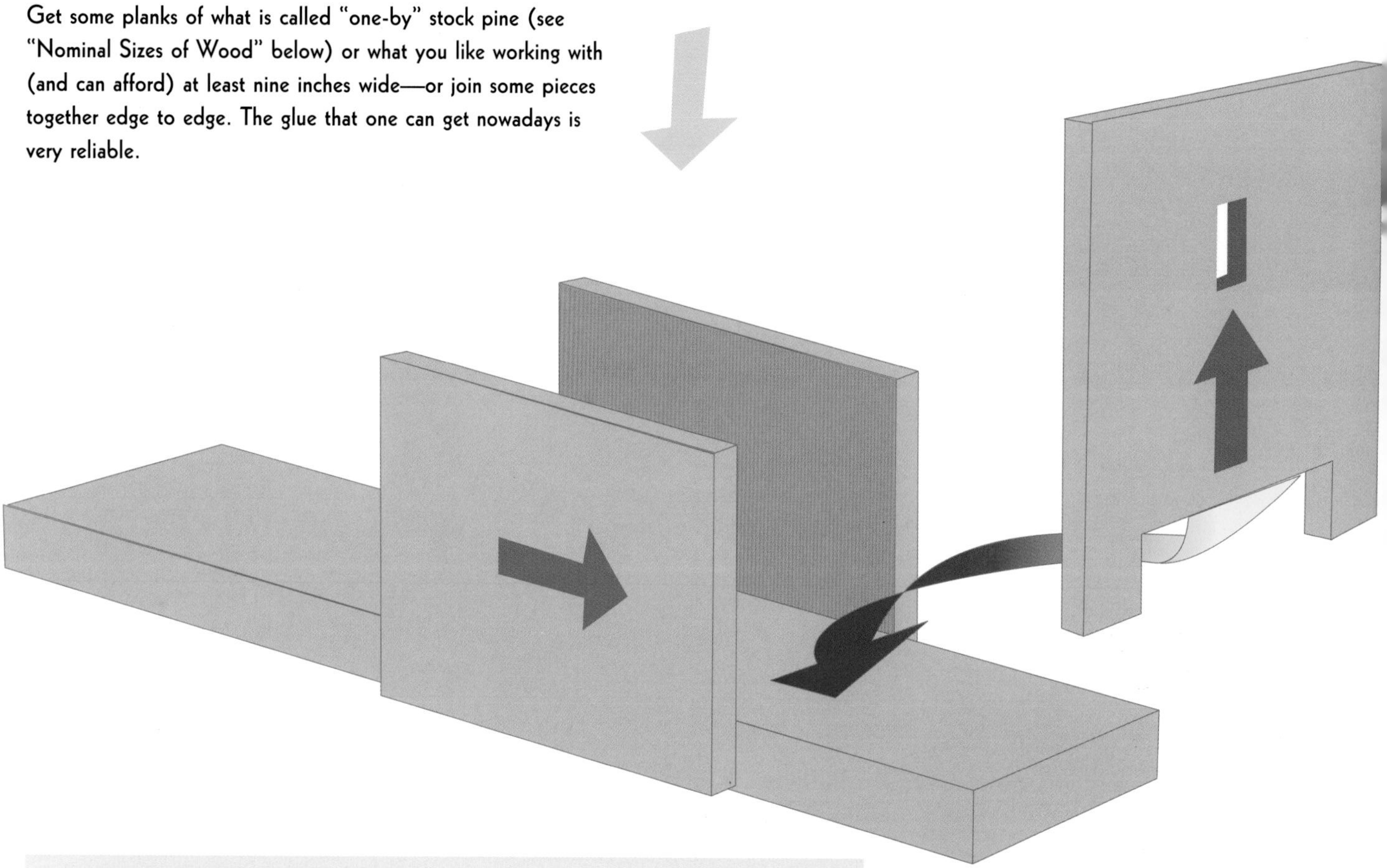

Nominal Sizes of Wood

Wood is sold in nominal sizes. A one-inch piece, called "one-by," is more like three quarters of an inch. You are not being ripped off by the lumberyard, it's just that they start measuring before it gets planed down smooth (dressed) and, because quite a bit of wood comes off, the wood is no longer as thick as it is called—if this is confusing, don't worry we've better things to think about.

The brown arrows on each piece tell you which way the grain should run. It can be made with the grain going in other directions depending on what kind of wood you are using, so don't get tense about it.

These pages are just to give you an idea of the overall structure. For scale drawings, see pages 22 through 25.

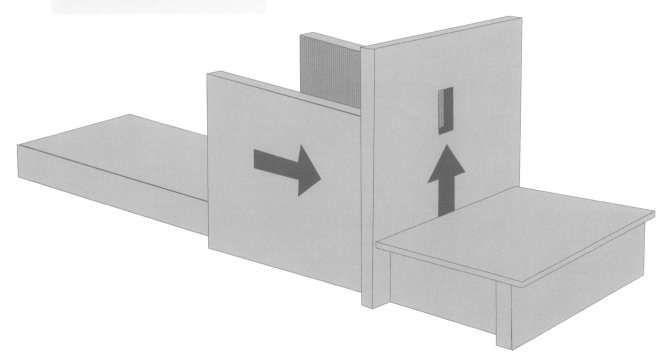

Apart from the base plank it would be quite suitable to make this from MDF (medium-density fiberboard). There is no edge screwing and the carving would be a lot easier.

Schematic Assembly

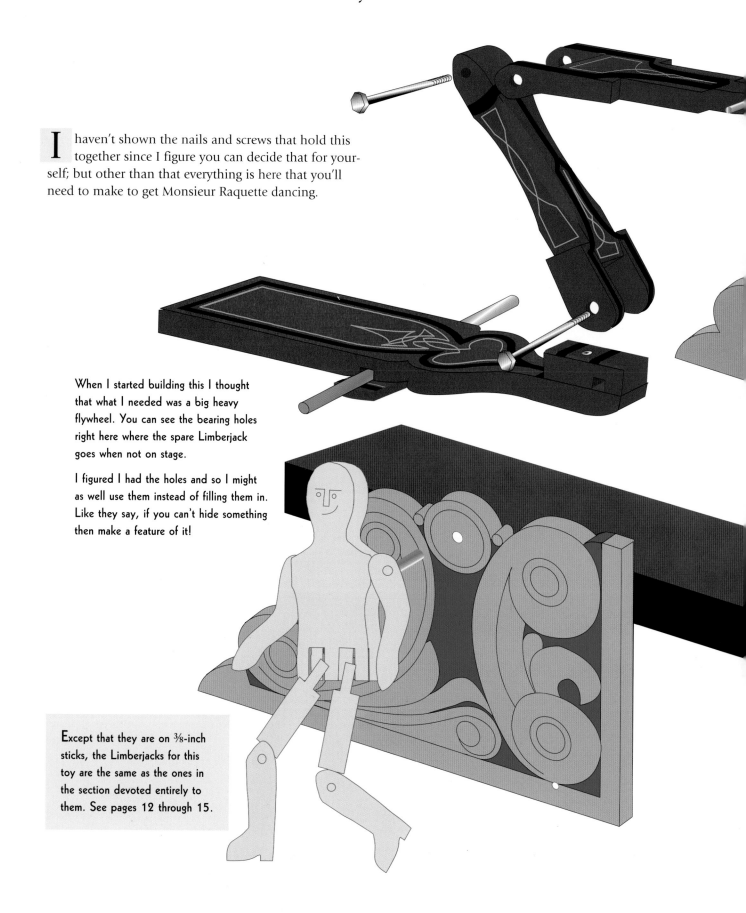

I haven't shown the nails and screws that hold this together since I figure you can decide that for yourself; but other than that everything is here that you'll need to make to get Monsieur Raquette dancing.

When I started building this I thought that what I needed was a big heavy flywheel. You can see the bearing holes right here where the spare Limberjack goes when not on stage.

I figured I had the holes and so I might as well use them instead of filling them in. Like they say, if you can't hide something then make a feature of it!

Except that they are on ⅜-inch sticks, the Limberjacks for this toy are the same as the ones in the section devoted entirely to them. See pages 12 through 15.

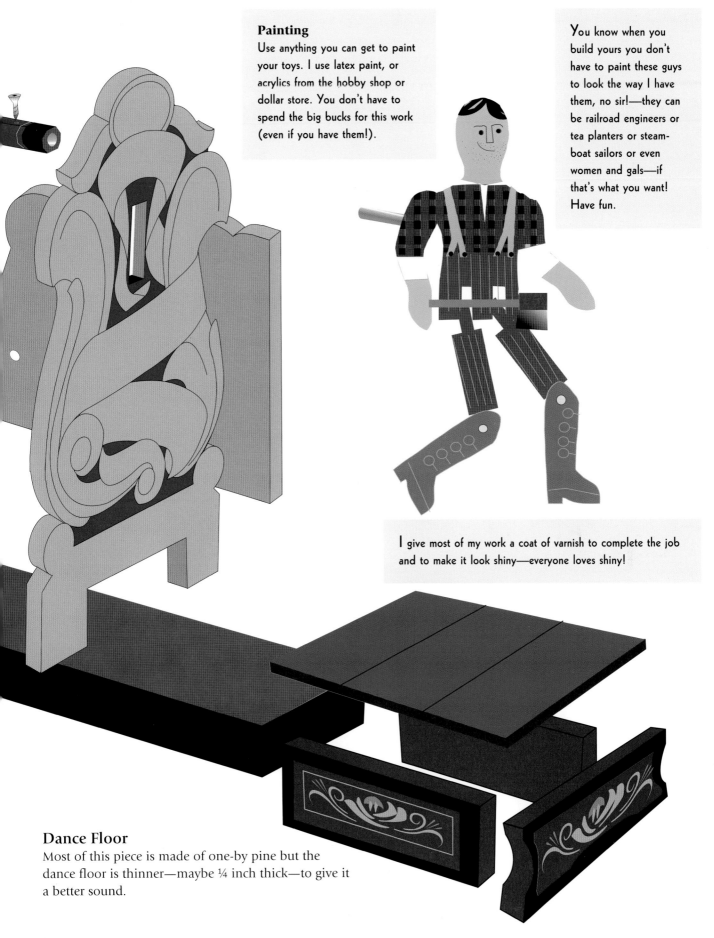

Painting

Use anything you can get to paint your toys. I use latex paint, or acrylics from the hobby shop or dollar store. You don't have to spend the big bucks for this work (even if you have them!).

You know when you build yours you don't have to paint these guys to look the way I have them, no sir!—they can be railroad engineers or tea planters or steamboat sailors or even women and gals—if that's what you want! Have fun.

I give most of my work a coat of varnish to complete the job and to make it look shiny—everyone loves shiny!

Dance Floor

Most of this piece is made of one-by pine but the dance floor is thinner—maybe ¼ inch thick—to give it a better sound.

P hotocopy (or draw) these up to full size, and transfer to some one-by stock. I'll leave it to you to decide how many pieces of each you'll need.

For the low relief carving trace the lines onto the wood and then, with a pocketknife, cut down on each line to a depth of about ⅛ inch. Bevel off one side and it looks real nice. Maybe practice just a little before hand on a piece of similar wood—don't practice too much!

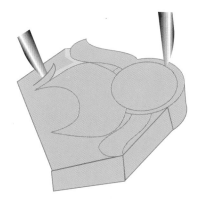

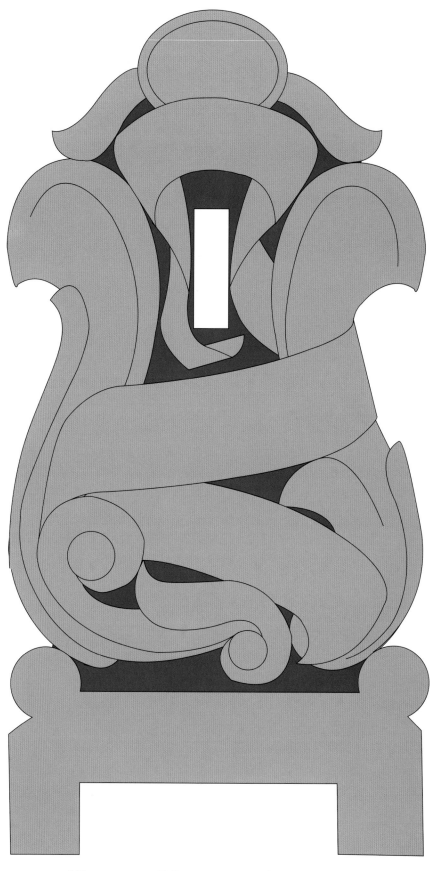

Listen, you don't have to carve this at all —just paint the decoration on; it's your toy. You decide.

Let me put that another way—you don't have to paint this toy, just carve it—it's your toy!

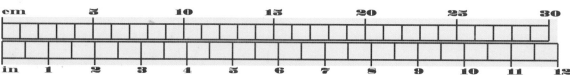

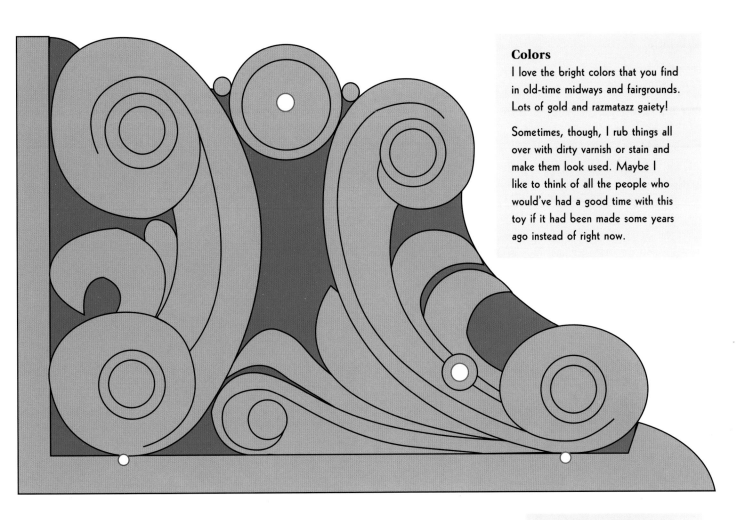

Colors
I love the bright colors that you find in old-time midways and fairgrounds. Lots of gold and razmatazz gaiety!

Sometimes, though, I rub things all over with dirty varnish or stain and make them look used. Maybe I like to think of all the people who would've had a good time with this toy if it had been made some years ago instead of right now.

Touch-up Painting
If you have to touch up the paint sometimes because kids have worn it off by winding (and they will!), don't fret over matching the color exactly. When fairground equipment has to be touched up on the road, instead of sending it back to the shop, they just paint it with whatever they've got. There is a special name for the effect, its called "park paint." If it's got a special name, it must be okay, says I.

Another thing I don't worry about is distress. My attitude is, if it gets dented or broken, it's all in fun and I'll fix it.

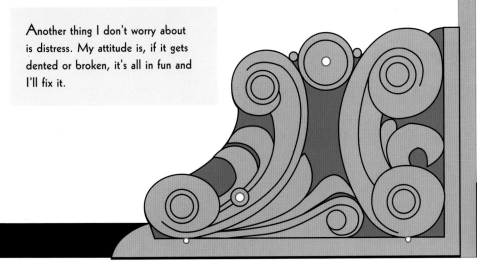

This view is one-quarter scale.

When you're with a group of people and your conversation lags, ask them what they consider to be the most important part of a car—or any complicated thing, really—fish, theodolites, human beings. You can get quite a heated discussion going.

Why I mentioned this is because right here on these pages are the most important parts of the Monsieur Raquette project, which, of course, is not true at all.

These pieces, though, are essential and it's good to get them as close as you can to what I have here.

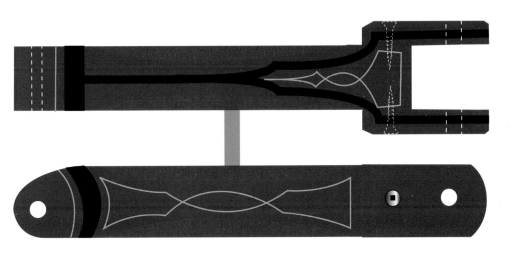

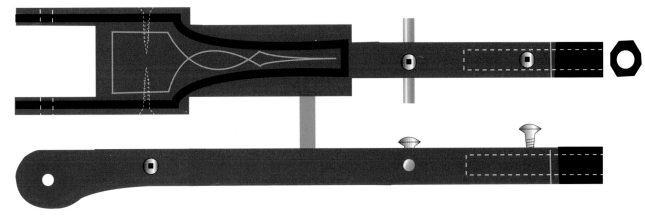

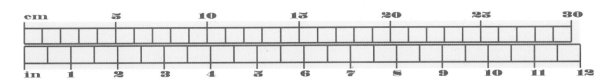

The Pianist,
Definitely Knot the Blues

Often, I'm asked why I started building these toys and I really don't know—I just have to do it. What I can say is that I do remember the day I started and what I made. I made this pianist. Why a pianist?—I don't know. I do know that when I had made this, I turned the handle and the magic happened. The little hands went up and down. I chuckled. I showed it to a friend. We laughed!

If you are looking for ideas, what I recommend is that you do a bit of "idea gardening." What is that? Well, go to the library. The library is a physical place. Rows of shelves. Different covers of many books. Find something you like. When you don't know what you like or are in a rut looking at the same thing all the time, do this: Wander around until you realize that you are in an area that you are unfamiliar with. Look around and find out what is on the shelves. Take down a book. Find one with pictures (they are generally the big ones). Look at the pictures; find out what's going on in the pictures. Your mind is like a cat (if it is out of practice teach it again). Watch a cat. Pretend that you are a cat and the pictures are a flock of birds. Act like a cat.

Here's another method—people generally leave books on the tables in libraries; pick up one or two and look through them. Find some pictures in them; a new search has begun.

Whatever method you use, after a while, sometimes a long while, you will, by study and enquiry and interests followed, find yourself back in the shelves that you are familiar with—but now you see what is in it with a new fresh eye. I say save the expression "been there, done that" for when you're dead!

When I go to a different town or district I find the library and look around. The shelves and book arrangements will be different and what is amazing is that they will have an almost entirely different set of books from your library. Explore, and enjoy yourself!

Scale Drawings & Details of Mechanism

Y ou've already noticed that the drawings on this page are a bit more glamorous than in the photo you've just seen. Well, I thought it would be good for you to see in the photo what these toys look like when they are just made. You know, they are fun even in plain wood; but with paint and varnish they can be even more full of character and fantasy.

On this page we can see the overall plans and elevations—when I am building these toys I have no drawings except for the occasional small scribble of the idea. (It's so simple a drawing that it's not even dignified enough to call it a sketch!) Why I'm telling you this is because maybe I've left out a little something and you may say, "now how do I make this, it doesn't say!" In situations like that—you decide. If it works, that's good; if your idea doesn't work—try again. If you keep on trying and nothing goes right— take a break. How long a break? Sometimes five minutes, sometimes an hour, maybe six months. Have a nice time.

The scale, shown below, will tell you that these drawings are shown at half size. This is, of course, not mandatory. You can make this toy at any size you want.

Don't limit yourself with other people's ideas!

Plan View

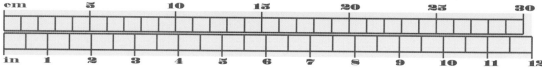

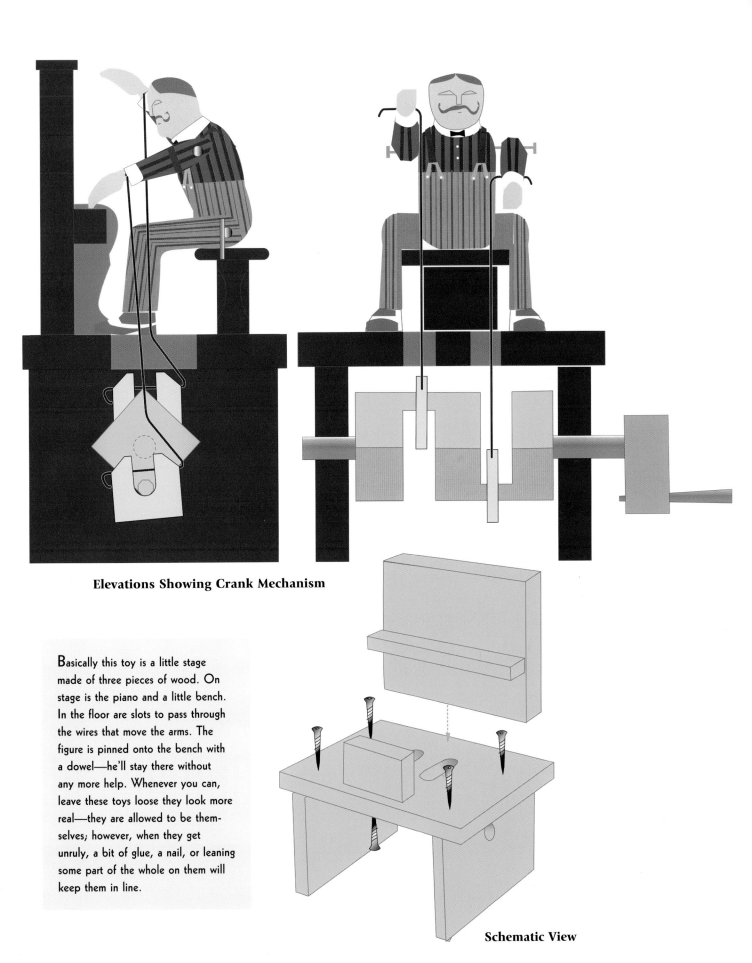

Elevations Showing Crank Mechanism

Basically this toy is a little stage made of three pieces of wood. On stage is the piano and a little bench. In the floor are slots to pass through the wires that move the arms. The figure is pinned onto the bench with a dowel—he'll stay there without any more help. Whenever you can, leave these toys loose they look more real—they are allowed to be themselves; however, when they get unruly, a bit of glue, a nail, or leaning some part of the whole on them will keep them in line.

Schematic View

Full Size

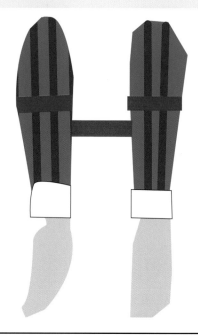

This pianist is done up real dude style. Make up your own style or naked is good too.

Paint is all it takes.

The diagram below shows how to run the grain in the legs and foot. The first diagram will work but it may be better to make the foot and leg separately.

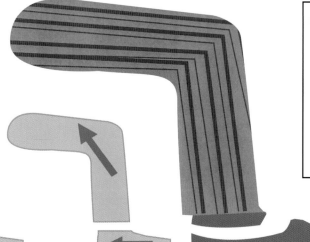

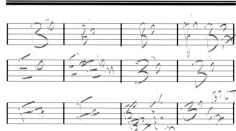

KNOT THE BLUES

Photocopy the keyboard and sheet music and glue in place.

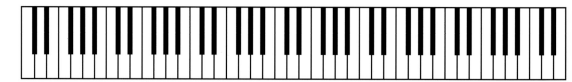

The maker's label is always fun to use. People think your work is more authentic if it has a printed label. Put your name in the slot provided—completely genuine!!

HOW TO CUT OUT THE CRANKSHAFT

Start with a block of one-and-a-half-inch-square stuff, and mark it out as shown. This can be very tricky, so don't rush.

Remember—if you make a mistake, just start over—there is absolutely no shame involved in that.

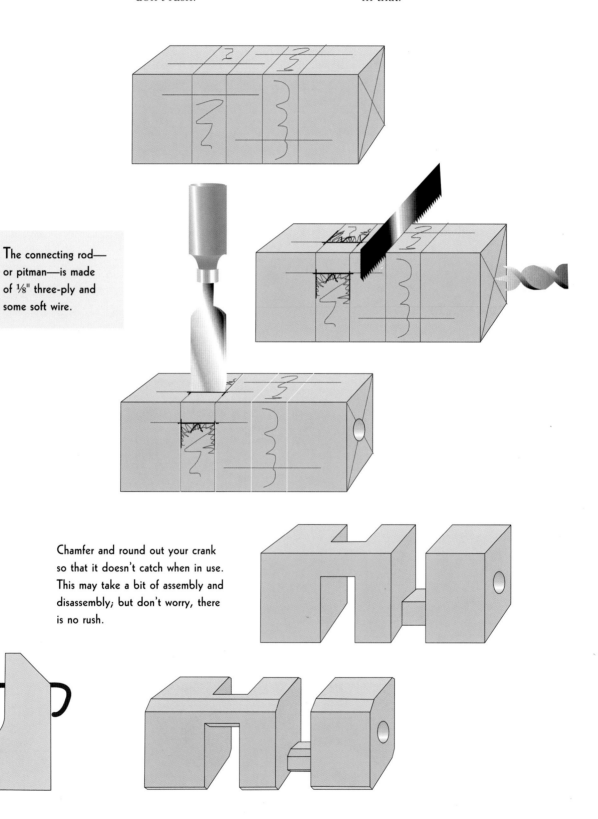

The connecting rod—or pitman—is made of ⅛" three-ply and some soft wire.

Chamfer and round out your crank so that it doesn't catch when in use. This may take a bit of assembly and disassembly; but don't worry, there is no rush.

Mr. Muscles
& Little Ms. Threemore

*S*tarting out as a joke is something that maybe we could all call "part of our heritage." This guy and gal continue to be a source of amusement. He more than she, perhaps, because of a happy accident. I had intended that he flex his muscles and show off; however, he went one further than this, and punched himself in the eye! He continues smiling nonetheless.

She is so serious that she is more of a mystery than a thing of fun. She is intent on doing her pushups. She has a bit of a grimace, but I figure that by now she has gotten the hang of it, so you can give her a big smile, if you prefer. These two started out on a whirligig, before I grew tired of waiting for a tropical storm or northeaster to get them moving, and instead converted them to finger power. I guess anyone would be serious after a lifestyle change like that!

The surprise element of them both is always fun. Mr. Muscles stands on a plinth and Ms. Threemore is on the ground, which is also a plinth. In front of the base is a finger hole for the operator. The finger depresses a lever and each goes into action. Ms. Threemore's pushups are entirely lever operated. Mr. Muscles has levers, wires, and a spring, which could be substituted with elastic. You could always make them back into whirligigs if you want an extra challenge; but then you have to wait around for the wind—when it blows. Wanting them to be able to spring into action whenever I wanted, rather than wait for the wind, probably had more to do with my moving away from traditional wind-driven machines to Whacky Toys than devising the mechanism for The Pianist.

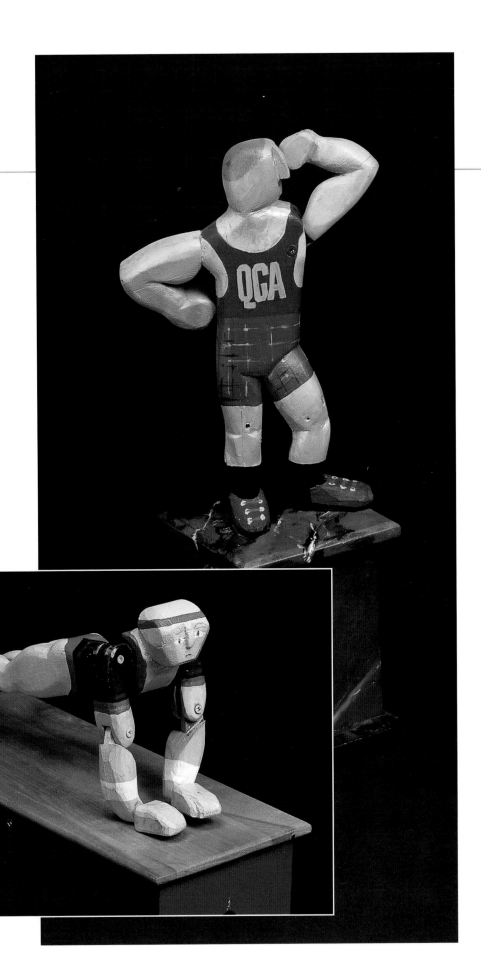

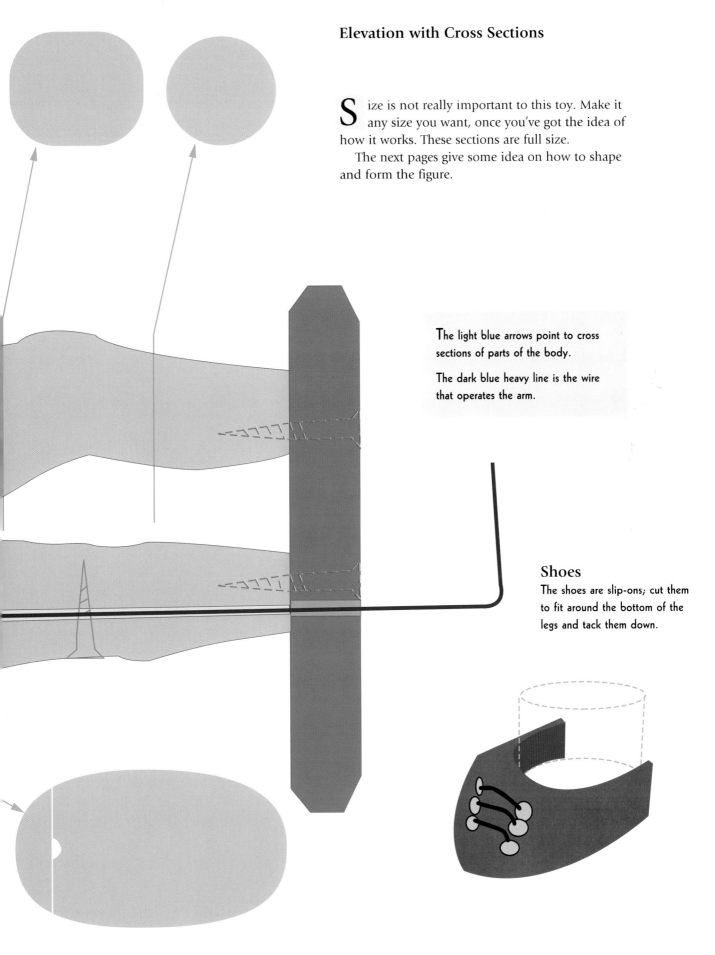

Elevation with Cross Sections

S ize is not really important to this toy. Make it any size you want, once you've got the idea of how it works. These sections are full size.

The next pages give some idea on how to shape and form the figure.

The light blue arrows point to cross sections of parts of the body.

The dark blue heavy line is the wire that operates the arm.

Shoes
The shoes are slip-ons; cut them to fit around the bottom of the legs and tack them down.

CARVING THE FIGURE OF MR. MUSCLES

Get the profile from page 34 —cut off all the corners and shape the figure to your liking.

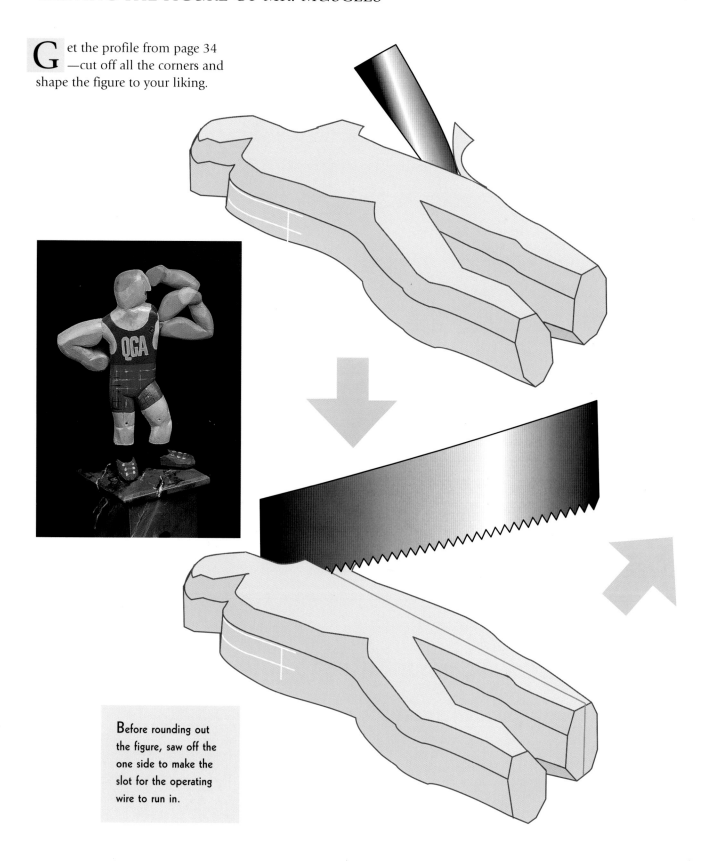

Before rounding out the figure, saw off the one side to make the slot for the operating wire to run in.

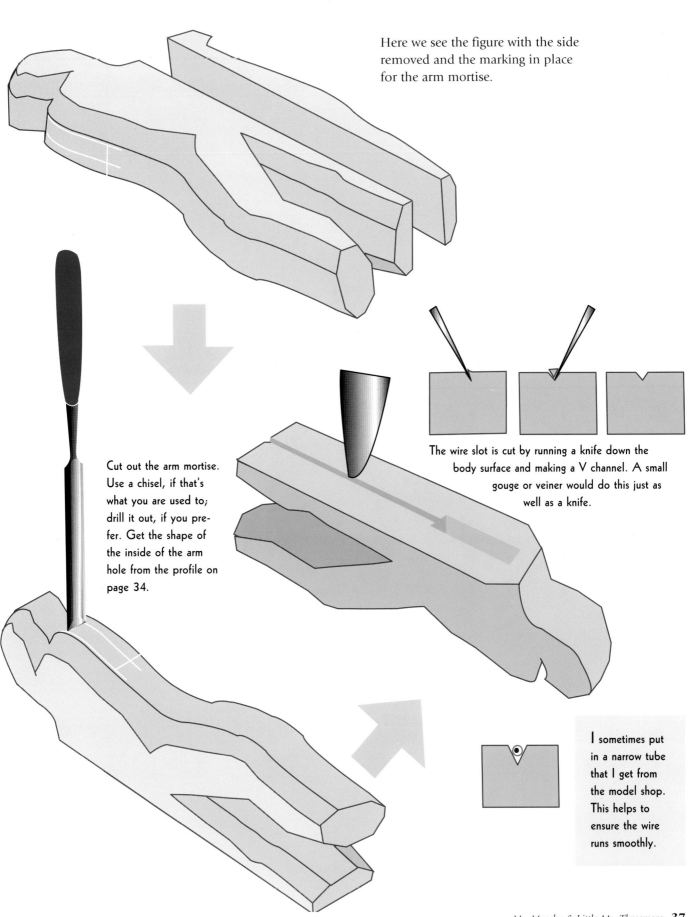

Here we see the figure with the side removed and the marking in place for the arm mortise.

Cut out the arm mortise. Use a chisel, if that's what you are used to; drill it out, if you prefer. Get the shape of the inside of the arm hole from the profile on page 34.

The wire slot is cut by running a knife down the body surface and making a V channel. A small gouge or veiner would do this just as well as a knife.

I sometimes put in a narrow tube that I get from the model shop. This helps to ensure the wire runs smoothly.

Schematic Drawings & Details of the Mechanism

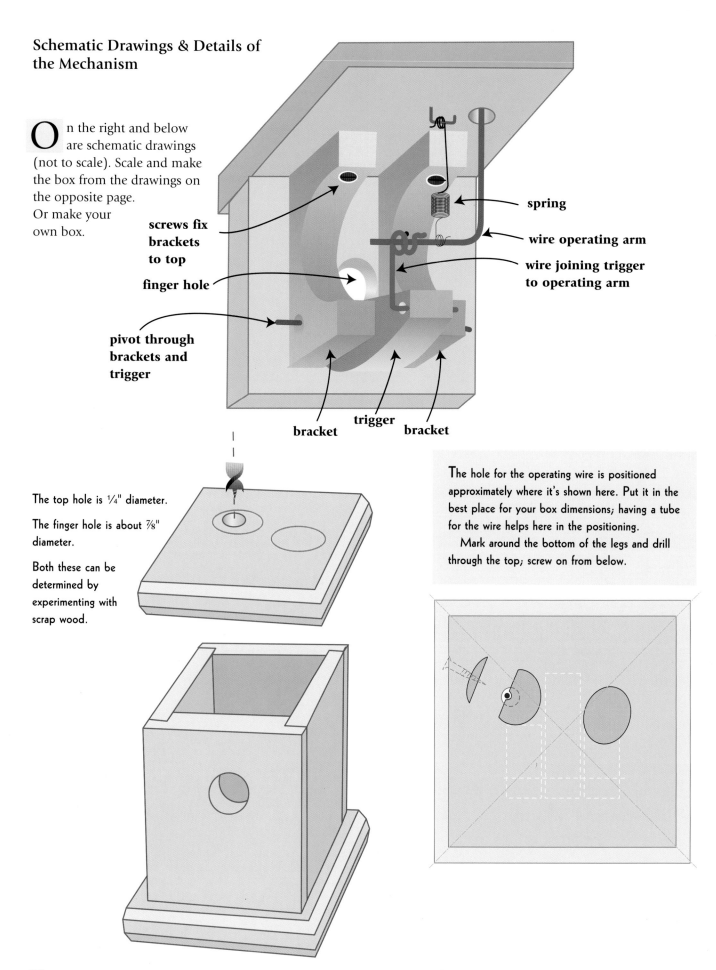

On the right and below are schematic drawings (not to scale). Scale and make the box from the drawings on the opposite page. Or make your own box.

screws fix brackets to top

finger hole

pivot through brackets and trigger

spring

wire operating arm

wire joining trigger to operating arm

bracket   **trigger**   **bracket**

The top hole is ¼" diameter.

The finger hole is about ⅞" diameter.

Both these can be determined by experimenting with scrap wood.

The hole for the operating wire is positioned approximately where it's shown here. Put it in the best place for your box dimensions; having a tube for the wire helps here in the positioning.

Mark around the bottom of the legs and drill through the top; screw on from below.

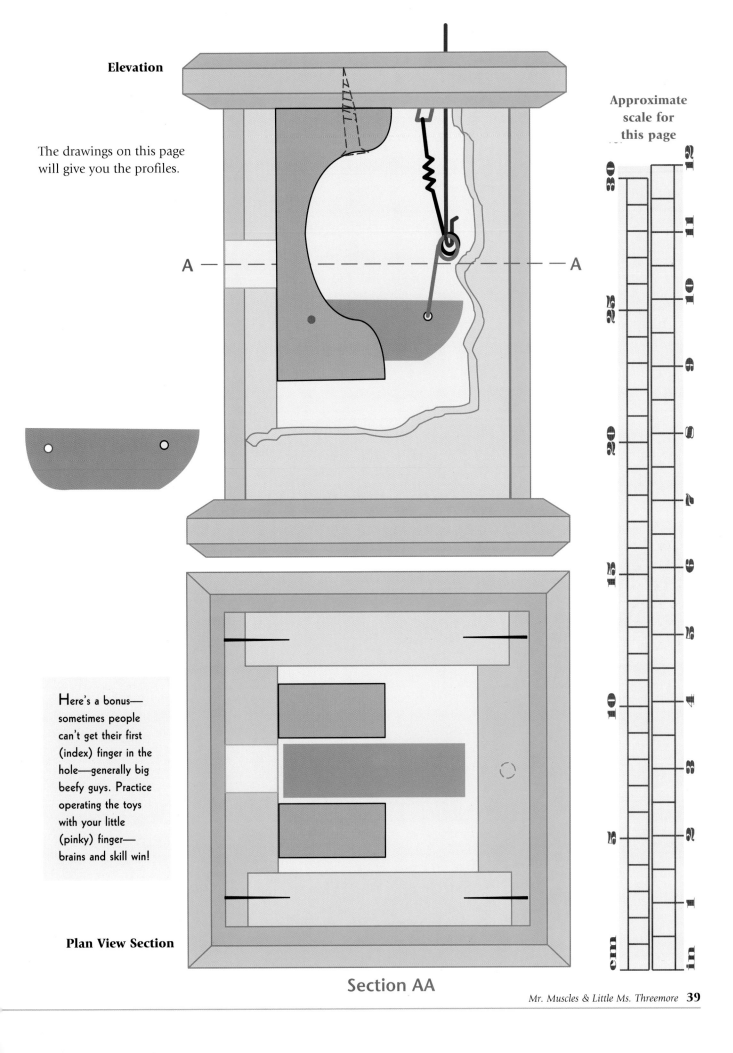

Elevation

The drawings on this page will give you the profiles.

A — — — — — — — — — — — — — A

Approximate scale for this page

Here's a bonus—sometimes people can't get their first (index) finger in the hole—generally big beefy guys. Practice operating the toys with your little (pinky) finger—brains and skill win!

Plan View Section

Section AA

LITTLE MS. THREEMORE

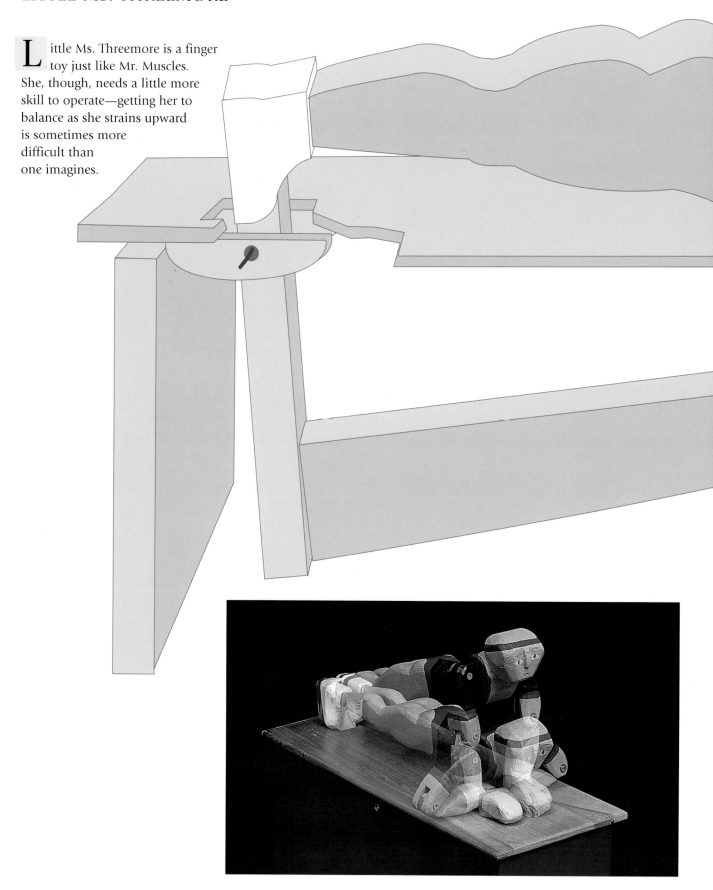

L ittle Ms. Threemore is a finger toy just like Mr. Muscles. She, though, needs a little more skill to operate—getting her to balance as she strains upward is sometimes more difficult than one imagines.

Schematic Drawings

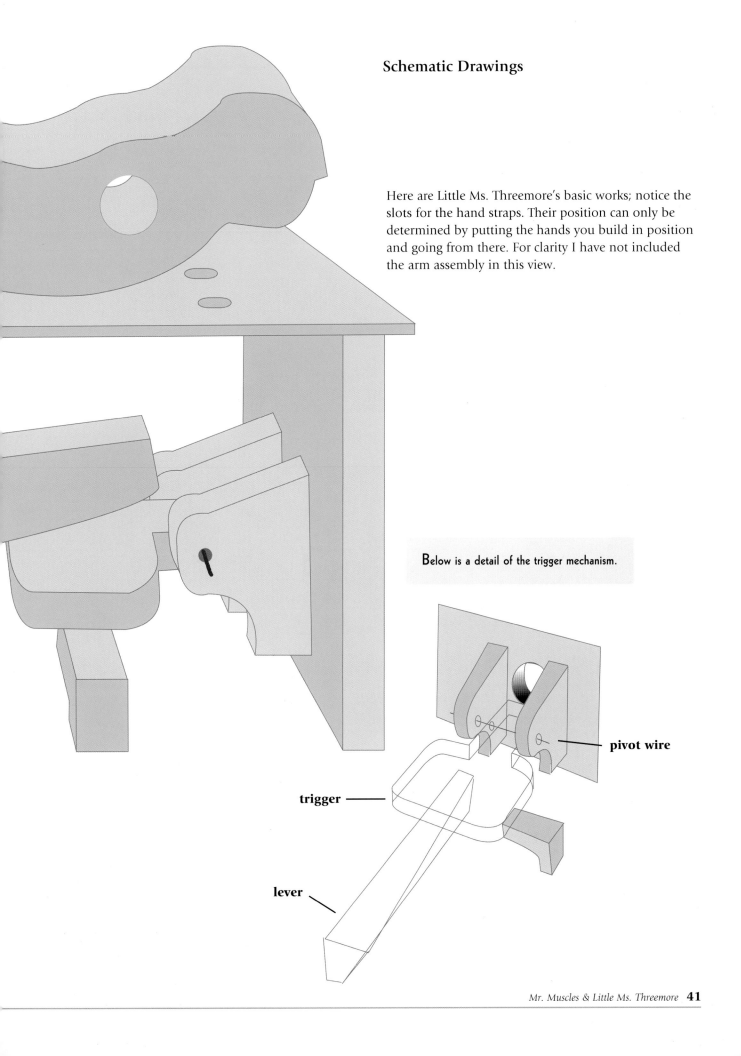

Here are Little Ms. Threemore's basic works; notice the slots for the hand straps. Their position can only be determined by putting the hands you build in position and going from there. For clarity I have not included the arm assembly in this view.

Below is a detail of the trigger mechanism.

pivot wire

trigger

lever

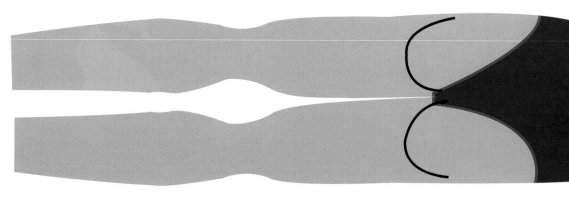

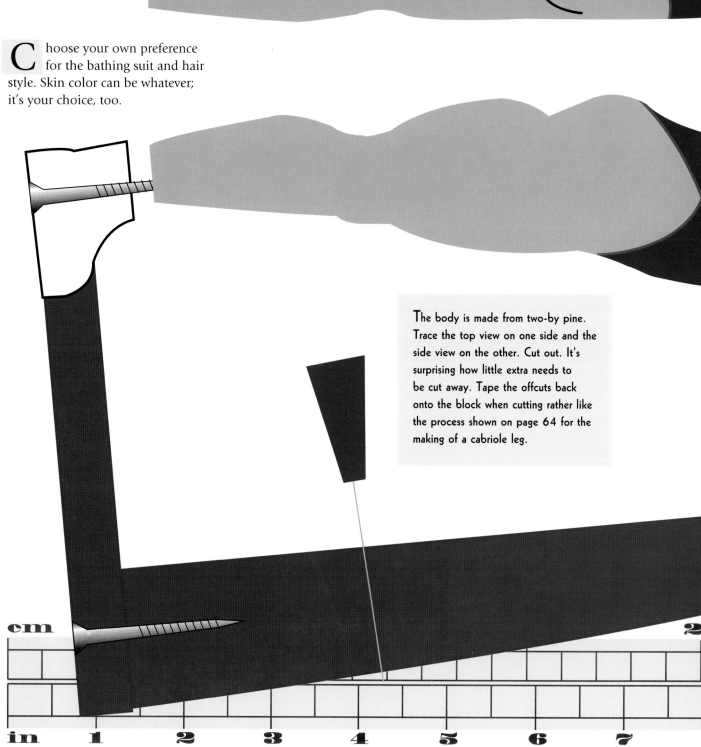

C hoose your own preference for the bathing suit and hair style. Skin color can be whatever; it's your choice, too.

The body is made from two-by pine. Trace the top view on one side and the side view on the other. Cut out. It's surprising how little extra needs to be cut away. Tape the offcuts back onto the block when cutting rather like the process shown on page 64 for the making of a cabriole leg.

cm   20

in   1   2   3   4   5   6   7

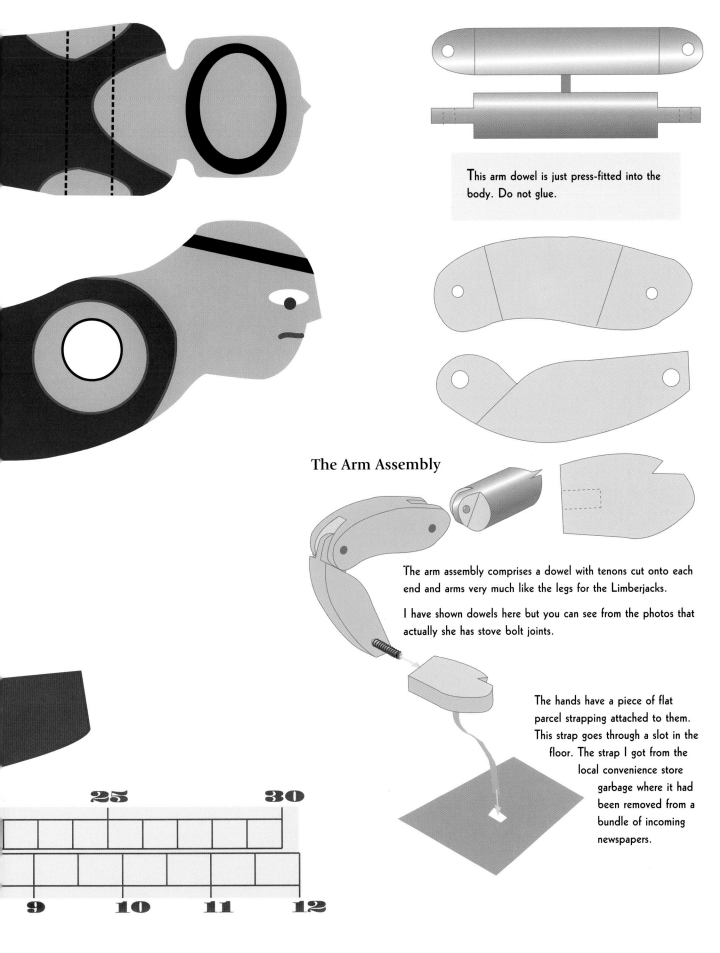

This arm dowel is just press-fitted into the body. Do not glue.

The Arm Assembly

The arm assembly comprises a dowel with tenons cut onto each end and arms very much like the legs for the Limberjacks.

I have shown dowels here but you can see from the photos that actually she has stove bolt joints.

The hands have a piece of flat parcel strapping attached to them. This strap goes through a slot in the floor. The strap I got from the local convenience store garbage where it had been removed from a bundle of incoming newspapers.

W hen making this toy, it will be best to make the mechanisms and then the floor; then build a box to suit what you have made. This route will help you later when you are making your own toys. Keep in mind that the box is part of the framework that helps support the mechanisms.

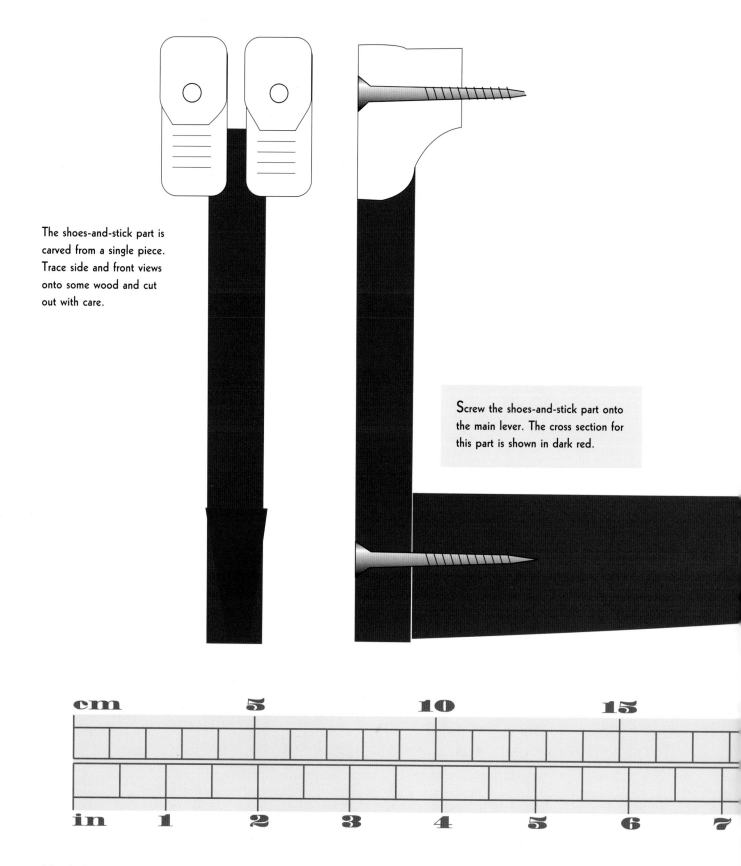

The shoes-and-stick part is carved from a single piece. Trace side and front views onto some wood and cut out with care.

Screw the shoes-and-stick part onto the main lever. The cross section for this part is shown in dark red.

cm 5 10 15

in 1 2 3 4 5 6 7

The Box

The box is joined to the lid (floor) by screws into blocks that have been glued to the underside of the floor.

The box is made of pine and painted to some available color. The floor came from some piece of ¼" maple I scrounged from the guy next door when he threw out some furniture.

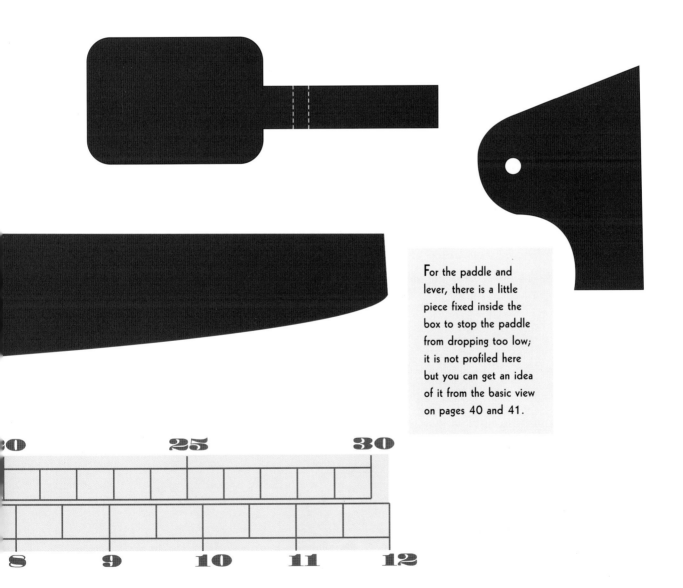

For the paddle and lever, there is a little piece fixed inside the box to stop the paddle from dropping too low; it is not profiled here but you can get an idea of it from the basic view on pages 40 and 41.

A Politically Correct Weather House

For such a simple toy this weather house sure has a lot of stories. For starters the name should give you the clue that a whole can of worms is attached or as my friend Stan used to say, "Well, that's the color of a different horse!" I hope that by the time you read this the insanity known as political correctness is obsolete, dead, and gone. If it is then this is what PC madness was all about. It was the crazy notion that if someone imagines that something might be offensive to them then everybody else has to be careful that they don't say or do something that aggravates those imaginings. That's the simple version of a complicated and miserable behavioral event. Good riddance!

Once I had the idea to build a little weather house. This is the result. No little guy in a sou'wester, no little lady in a bonnet with flowers, no cute house with little doors—afterall that would be politically incorrect; no stereotypical characterizations allowed—but it works and you have to use your memory, which is often a good thing!

Politically Correct Hygrometer No. 6

How to use your weather house

Setting up the PCH
Put the house in a totally sheltered environment. A completely dust, speck and mote free situation is preferred.

Using the PCH
Your weather house comes complete with two unprepossessing nonethnic male type figures. When one or the other comes out of the house, as if leaving—things will be good.

The Politically Correct Weather House will give many years of service if nurtured.

Office use only
Made by
Designed by
Inspected by

Sex ☐ M ☐ F   Age___
Needed help in completing ☐ yes ☐ no

MADE IN CANADA

SCALE DRAWING

All the parts here are shown at about 50%. Scale it, if that's what you like to do, or photocopy it up to 200%. As with most of the toys in this book, dimensions are often not critical. Bigger, smaller, eyeball it, try it—make it work the way it wants.

The materials that you use will influence a lot of the sizes and will eventually, combined with your own personal preferences, likes and dislikes for shapes and sizes, help you create your own style and pieces.

The weight at the end of the string is from some old plumbing parts—anything similar will do just as well.

I made this thing in about an hour; it took me about a year to find the old tennis racket one day in a garbage can while out walking. I was very excited at the discovery.

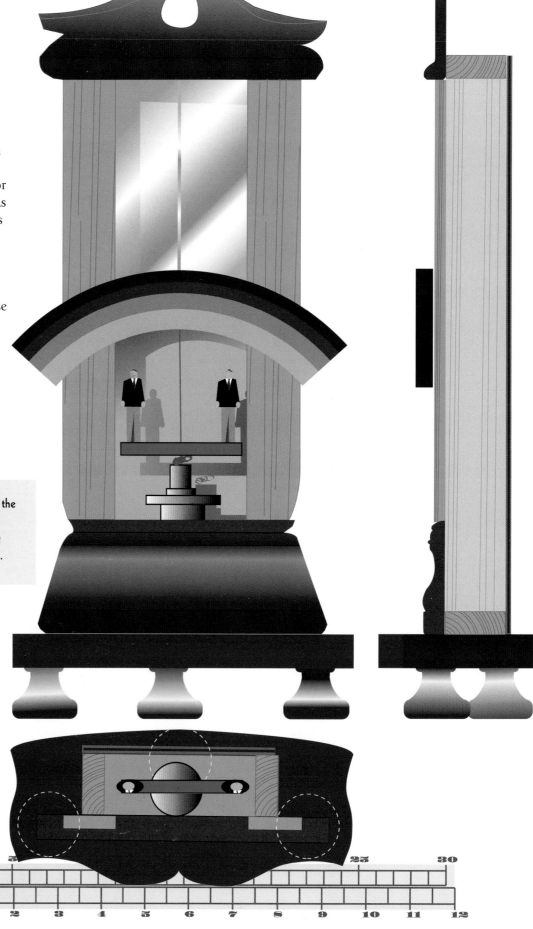

Plan View

MAKING THE BOX

Make a simple and longish box and add all the other parts: a stand, to help it be upright; feet, if you want, and so on.

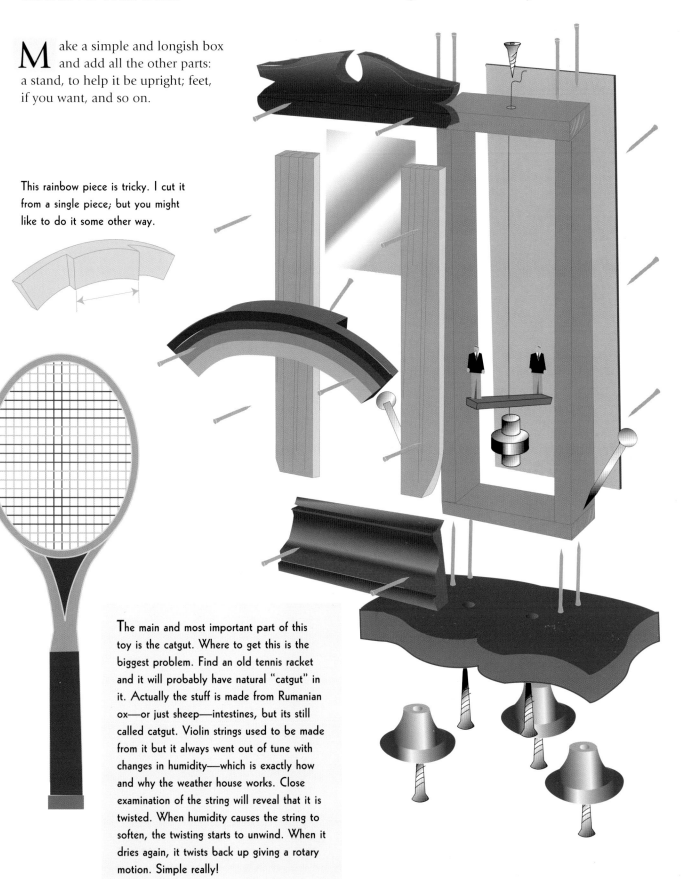

This rainbow piece is tricky. I cut it from a single piece; but you might like to do it some other way.

The main and most important part of this toy is the catgut. Where to get this is the biggest problem. Find an old tennis racket and it will probably have natural "catgut" in it. Actually the stuff is made from Rumanian ox—or just sheep—intestines, but its still called catgut. Violin strings used to be made from it but it always went out of tune with changes in humidity—which is exactly how and why the weather house works. Close examination of the string will reveal that it is twisted. When humidity causes the string to soften, the twisting starts to unwind. When it dries again, it twists back up giving a rotary motion. Simple really!

Granddad's Helper, a Whirligig

*C*hopping wood and stopping trains with a swinging lantern I'd seen too many times in whirligigs. I can't remember the last time I got kicked by a cow (that other whirligig favorite), but I do use a drawknife a lot. So why not a Sunday Toy with someone on a shaving horse using a drawknife; why not?

Why not indeed—so I started. And after I was getting into it, thinking that things couldn't get any better, Dhyani, my granddaughter, came to visit! She likes to smile and help that way—by just being around. It's comfortable having her close and so that's how she came to be in this toy. We have lots of loving fun being out there, together in all weathers.

I made this toy as a self portrait some years ago. I'm a lot younger now and Dhyani is really growing up into a lovely lady.

What do you like to do? Make a whirligig of it! Why not? There are many ways to solve simple problems of movement and this toy makes use of a direct crankshaft linked by two connecting rods to the body of granddad; the legs are fixed so it is the back and forth of granddad using the shaving horse that creates the movement. But, of course, I couldn't do it without my little helper!

W hen I started to make this toy I took two pieces of one-and-a-half-inch pine about 2 feet long and joined them at the ends by pieces about 4 inches wide. I built the little bench, and added the guy (me).

As usual, try fiddling this one 'til it works. What's here is the principle of the thing. When making these toys, I generally allow for adjustments. A good example is the dowel that activates the guy—it has a screw to make other settings— you'll need this. The plank that he is "cutting" is adjustable too so a finishing nail will be enough to hold it.

Schematic Drawing of Shaving Horse Assembly

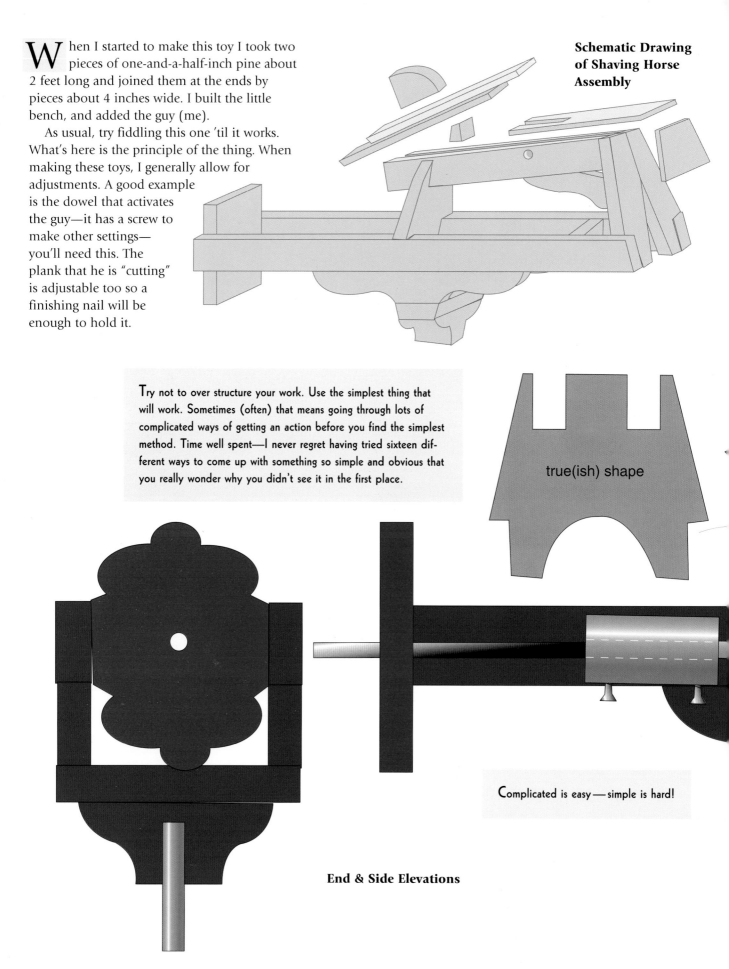

Try not to over structure your work. Use the simplest thing that will work. Sometimes (often) that means going through lots of complicated ways of getting an action before you find the simplest method. Time well spent—I never regret having tried sixteen different ways to come up with something so simple and obvious that you really wonder why you didn't see it in the first place.

true(ish) shape

Complicated is easy—simple is hard!

End & Side Elevations

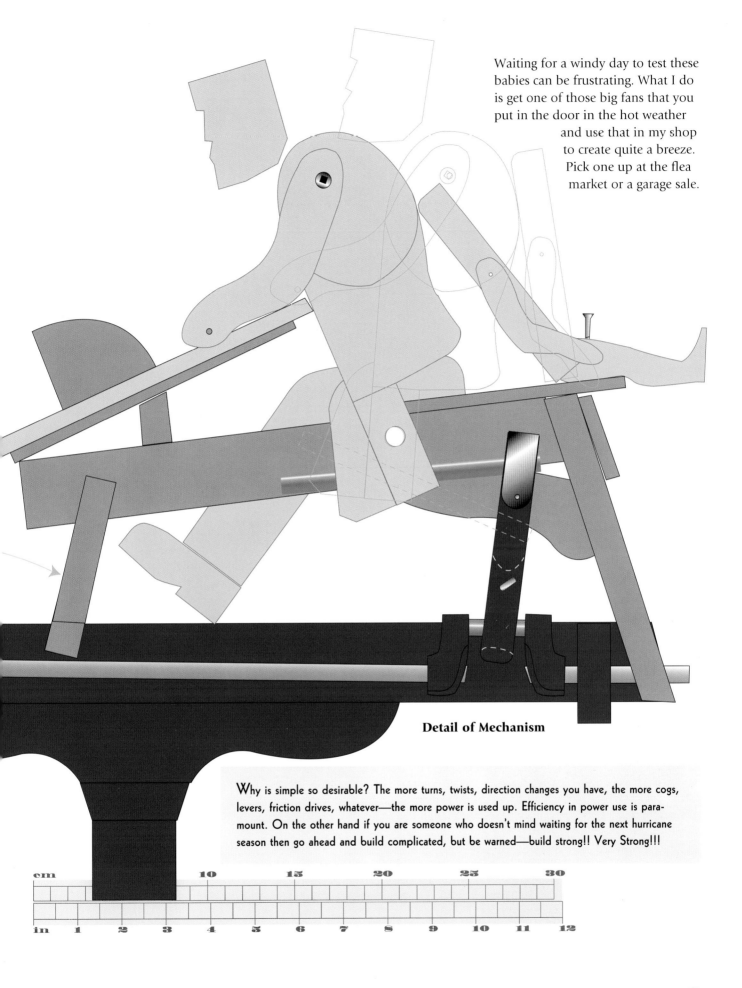

Waiting for a windy day to test these babies can be frustrating. What I do is get one of those big fans that you put in the door in the hot weather and use that in my shop to create quite a breeze. Pick one up at the flea market or a garage sale.

Detail of Mechanism

Why is simple so desirable? The more turns, twists, direction changes you have, the more cogs, levers, friction drives, whatever—the more power is used up. Efficiency in power use is paramount. On the other hand if you are someone who doesn't mind waiting for the next hurricane season then go ahead and build complicated, but be warned—build strong!! Very Strong!!!

cm 10 15 20 25 30

in 1 2 3 4 5 6 7 8 9 10 11 12

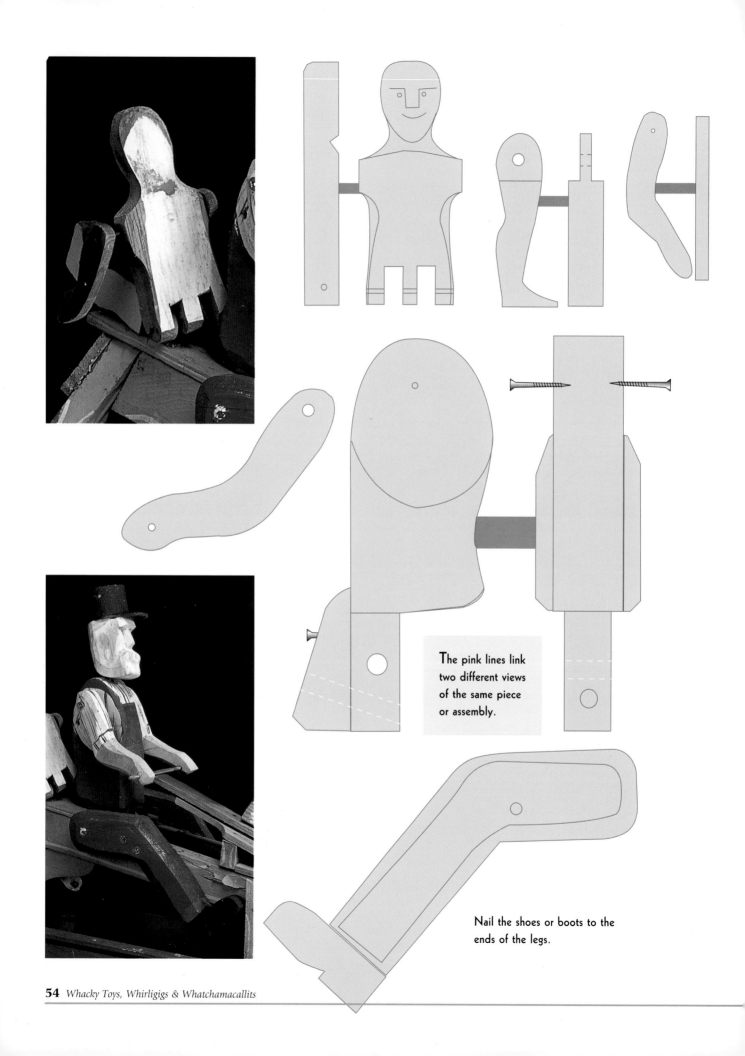

The pink lines link two different views of the same piece or assembly.

Nail the shoes or boots to the ends of the legs.

HOW TO MAKE A PIECE WORK

This connecting rod—or pitman, as they are sometimes called; the odd looking piece in red with the oval hole—is a good example of the way I work. The wire is there to make the hole a bit smaller. Maybe if you make this toy you could try making the hole smaller instead of using a wire. Let me say just this—if I were to make this whirligig toy again I'd make a smaller hole, but it might not work. So I'd keep at it 'til it did work. Which is another good example of the way I work.

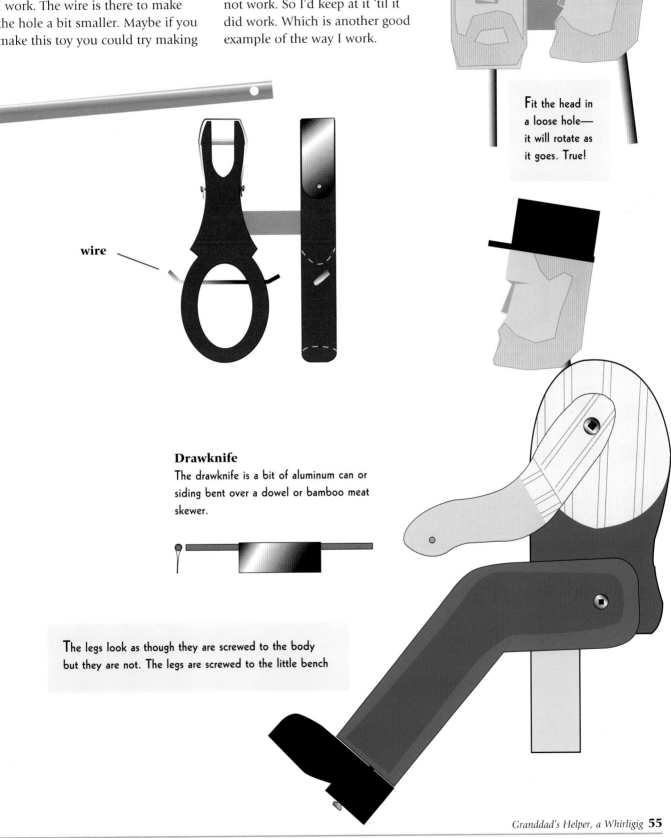

Fit the head in a loose hole— it will rotate as it goes. True!

wire

Drawknife
The drawknife is a bit of aluminum can or siding bent over a dowel or bamboo meat skewer.

The legs look as though they are screwed to the body but they are not. The legs are screwed to the little bench

Granddad's Night Out, a Dancing Phenomenon

*S*urprise yourself and bring up a few memories. I started this toy as a relief from doing woodwork—you buy a book called Whacky Toys, Whirligigs & Whatchamacallits *and you expect to hear something sensible? Anyhow, yes, I built a machine for those not skillful enough to work a limberjack.*

People are always asking the same old question, "How long did it take you to make this?"—you'll get it too after you've made some of these toys! Well for once I have an answer—I designed and built this one in one day. It's perfectly true! I was kind of proud of this until I started getting the feeling back from these same folks. "Oh, so it's not as much of an accomplishment as it looks."

Based on an actual event this toy has something for me to tell beyond just when I made it or how long it took to make when people ask. If you make yours based on some special event in your life (real or imagined) then it makes for more fun and also gives you a sense of purpose and meaning while you are making it.

W hen I first made this toy I had a guy in overalls as the doll. It was a self portrait; then I remembered something that happened to me and the whole scene changed. The story (a good one) is at the top of page 68.

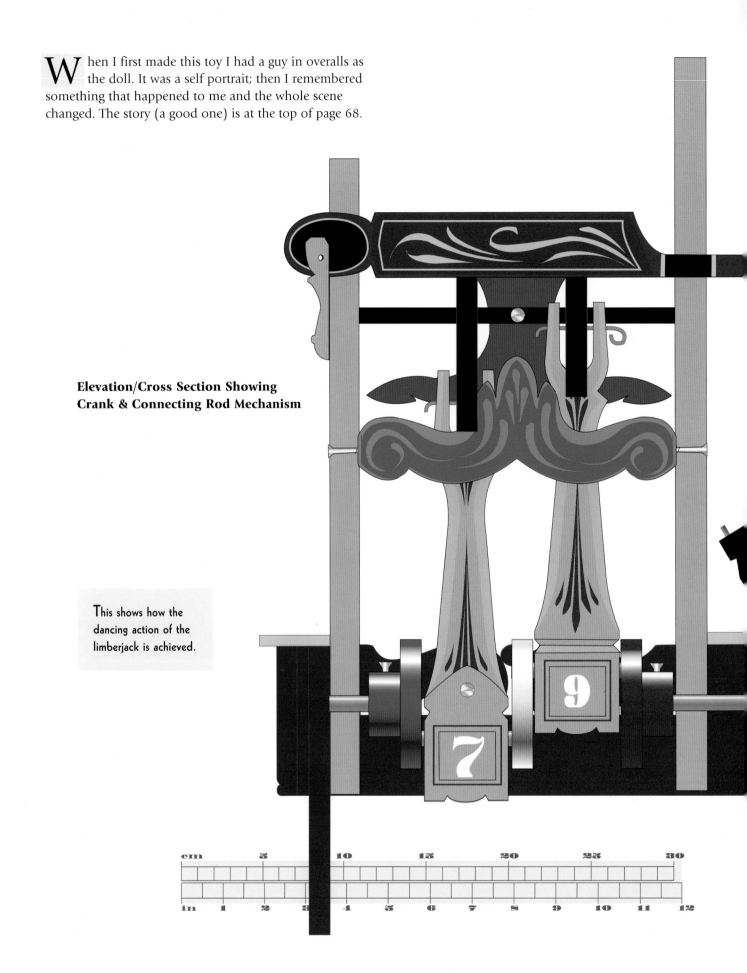

Elevation/Cross Section Showing Crank & Connecting Rod Mechanism

This shows how the dancing action of the limberjack is achieved.

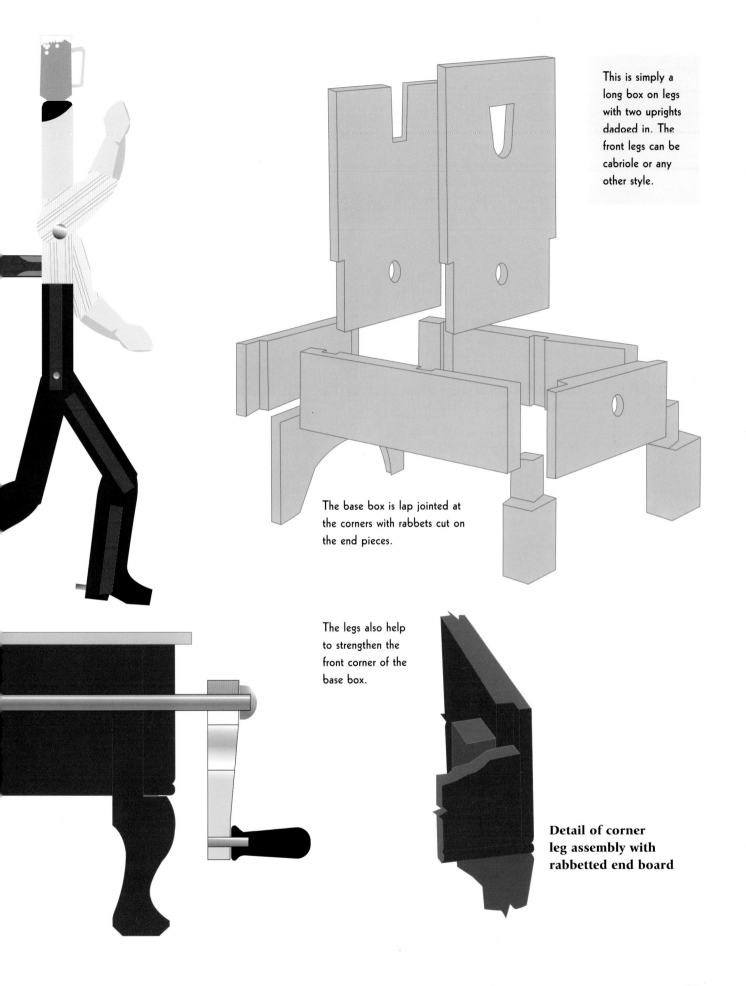

This is simply a long box on legs with two uprights dadoed in. The front legs can be cabriole or any other style.

The base box is lap jointed at the corners with rabbets cut on the end pieces.

The legs also help to strengthen the front corner of the base box.

Detail of corner leg assembly with rabbetted end board

H ere is the front view and a view with the Limber-jack doll and stage removed. I used ¾" sign board for the uprights. MDF (medium-density fiberboard) would be good since there is no side screwing—which is not good for MDF. One could also, if using MDF, carve decoration instead of only painting it on. This would give a very rich effect—very theatrical!

Some people think that a person who puts things together and then takes them apart and then puts them together again is some kind of a whimp—well not me!

When you are working at an experiment such as making crank toys that's all a necessary part of the process. I think this whole idea of not taking things apart comes from the dolts who can only follow instructions—they never can actually create anything themselves and they don't feel too good about themselves so they try to make you feel stupid because you work empirically (which is a simple way of saying—try it and see if it works and if it doesn't then try something a bit different until it does). This leads us to the conundrum: if we learn by making mistakes then the more mistakes we make, the more we know. What a mystery!

P atterns for this Limberjack doll are on pages 68 and 69.

Front Elevations

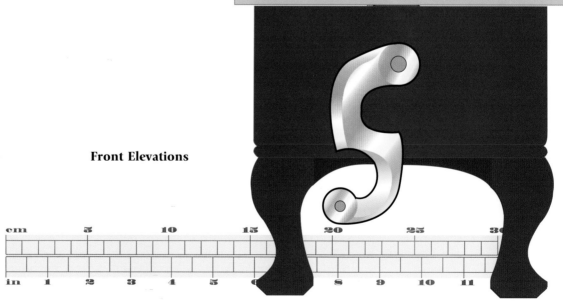

Painting

The painting decoration is only partially shown here. Make up your own decoration; be wild, be calm. It's up to you. Use any kind of paint. I use latex paint or acrylics. You don't have to paint yours to look the way mine does. Have fun.

I give most of my work a coat of varnish to complete the job and to make it look shiny—everyone loves shiny! Sometimes, I just rub things all over with dirty varnish or stain. This makes the toys look well used.

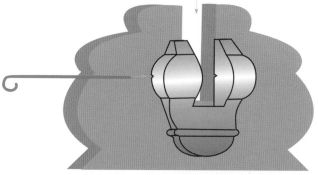

T he back end shoe is made from a piece of stock molding. One can get some interesting and surprising effects by cutting profiles on this easily obtained material.

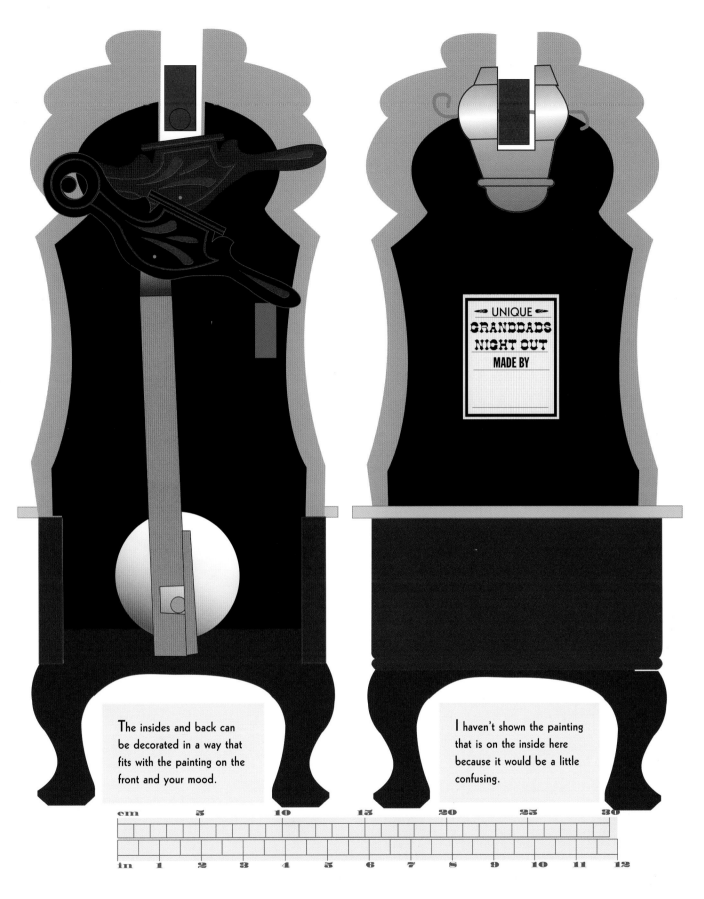

The insides and back can be decorated in a way that fits with the painting on the front and your mood.

I haven't shown the painting that is on the inside here because it would be a little confusing.

UNIQUE
GRANDDADS
NIGHT OUT
MADE BY

cm 5 10 15 20 25 30

in 1 2 3 4 5 6 7 8 9 10 11 12

Cross Section & Back Elevation

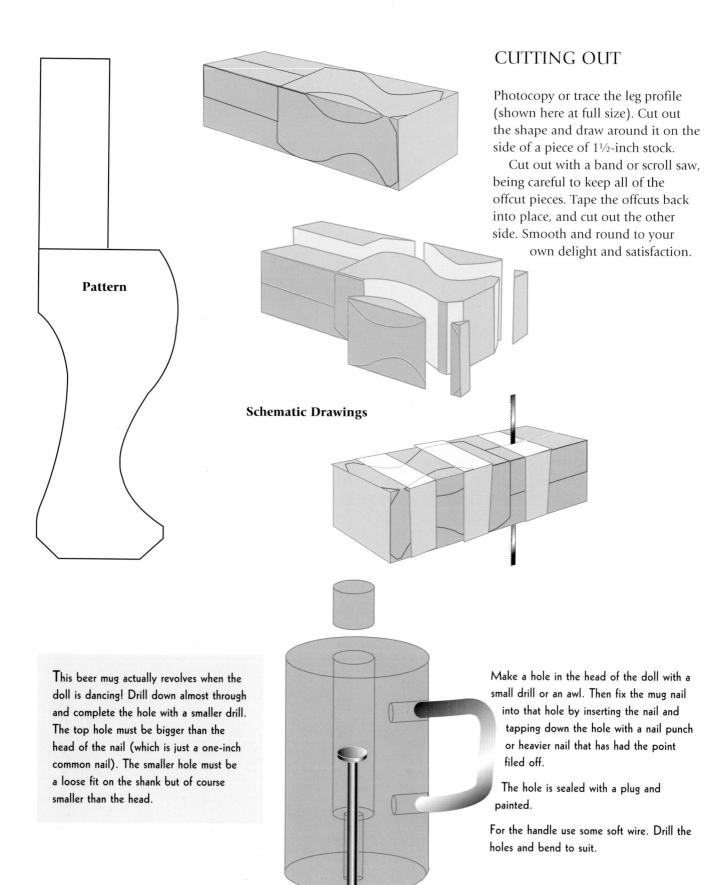

Pattern

CUTTING OUT

Photocopy or trace the leg profile (shown here at full size). Cut out the shape and draw around it on the side of a piece of 1½-inch stock.

Cut out with a band or scroll saw, being careful to keep all of the offcut pieces. Tape the offcuts back into place, and cut out the other side. Smooth and round to your own delight and satisfaction.

Schematic Drawings

This beer mug actually revolves when the doll is dancing! Drill down almost through and complete the hole with a smaller drill. The top hole must be bigger than the head of the nail (which is just a one-inch common nail). The smaller hole must be a loose fit on the shank but of course smaller than the head.

Make a hole in the head of the doll with a small drill or an awl. Then fix the mug nail into that hole by inserting the nail and tapping down the hole with a nail punch or heavier nail that has had the point filed off.

The hole is sealed with a plug and painted.

For the handle use some soft wire. Drill the holes and bend to suit.

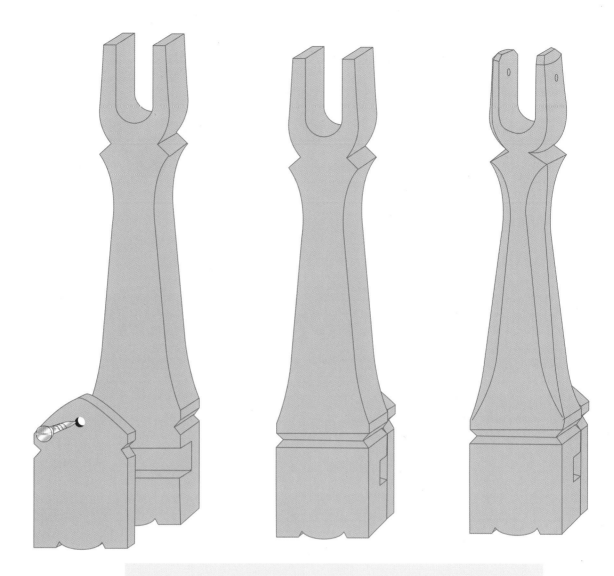

The connecting rods—or pitmen, as they are called in some parts of the world—can be a pretty elegant thing. Decorate them as you will; paint, carving, all okay as long as it doesn't interfere with the workings. These here are typical of my system. The main part is cut from ¾" stock and a cover from ¼" works well and enables removal when needed and during construction experiments and trying out.

Sides are cut away to give a more interesting profile and to enable the machinery mechanism to be seen. Shown here at half size.

MAKING THE CRANKSHAFT

Crankshafts can be a bit of a problem if they are not in line with themselves—that is, if the centers at each end are not in line and parallel.

I use this method to make crank systems:

Make some disks with a common center.

Fix them together and drill a hole for one of the crank pins.

Insert a piece of dowel to hold the discs in position and drill the other crank-pin hole.

Assemble the disks on a dowel that represents the shaft. Do not fix or glue.

Insert the dowels for the crank pins. Glue and pin them. Make sure that they are all in one plane.

When the glue is set, use a coping saw or tenon saw to saw away the unneeded parts of the crank pins.

Collars are glued to the ends to give support to the axles. The dowels in them, shown here, are only temporary. Make sure that they are not glued to the collars— perhaps by rubbing a little petroleum jelly (Vaseline) on them before inserting.

When the glue has set, drill for locking screws. Paint in whatever manner you want.

THE STORY BEHIND THIS CRANK TOY

People like to dance—it's only recently that in our Western society it's considered strange for men to dance together in groups. Large groups of men have always had some kind of togetherness thing, some dance together—Greeks are probably the most famous, Tutsi warriors are right up there too. The British army even has a musical event—it's naughty and it's fun! It's a strip tease called "These Old Boots of Mine." I don't know the full history of it (I'd like to though) but the special event goes like this:

A soldier gets up on stage at a dinner or likely gathering and sings "These old boots of mine. The insides is quite fine, the outsides have seen some stormy weather!—So I'll take these boots of mine and I'll hang 'em on the line (removes boots and hangs on something nearby). Roll on the boat that takes me home!"

He continues until he is completely naked. Verses are almost all the same except for the naming of each item of clothing. The audience joins in with the "Roll on the" chorus for a boisterous bit of fun.

I first saw this performed when I was a gunner in the Royal Artillery; my Dad, the Regimental Sergeant Major, was the performer!

As I said at the beginning, make your toys personal, it's more fun. And then you'll have agreat story to tell when someone asks you how old your toy is and how did you think it all up. It's all part of the fun, And it's a bit of magic!

I designed and made this during a really wild thunderstorm!

This Limberjack doll is shown at full size.

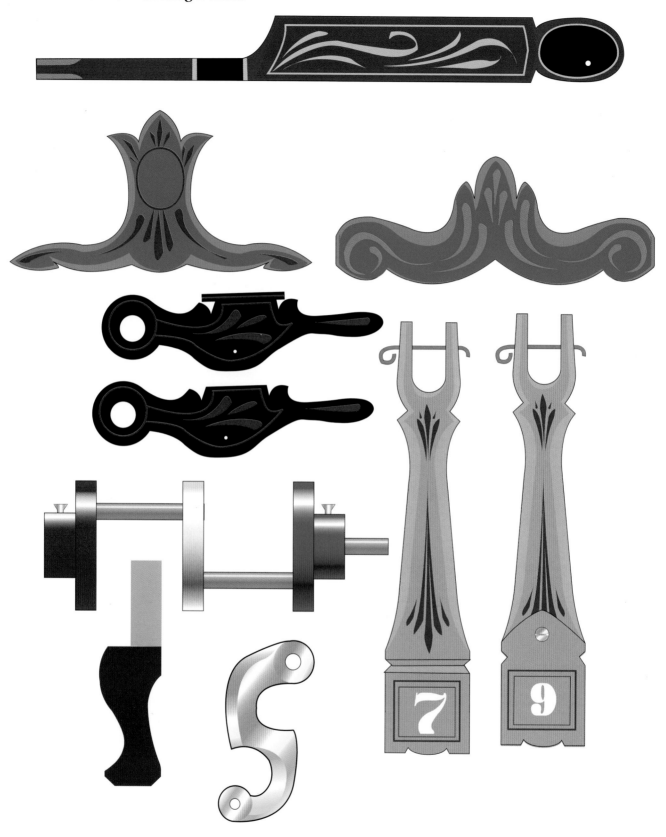

Midwinter Mnemonic

After a while making whacky toys helps you realize the truth—that it's the world that's whacky. Whacky toys seem to reflect it, they come into being because of it and, when they are done, the people in the "real" whacky world say, "Crazy! Where do you come up with your ideas?"

Midwinter Mnemonic came about like this. I was at a TV studio doing a spot about my book, The Nature of Woodworking. *Waiting for a cup of tea, I enquired about a box of nice wood pieces close to the door. It was, I was told, scrap for the garbage. I said that I could work for a whole week with a box of stuff like that and they invited me to be on the "what-you-can-do-with-scraps" show. "We will deliver the scrap," they said and did. The wood was delivered by the producer some weeks later leaving me about two weeks to do something—but that was no problem. The scrap was delivered to my front room by the producer and I put the question to him, "What . . . ?" but once rid of the scrap (I guess to him this was like garbage detail) he wanted out of my place—fast!*

"What's the show about?" I called as he hurried down the garden path. "What's the theme—furniture, toys, what?" I hollered as he slammed the truck door shut.

Turning as he hit the pedal to the metal—"Make one of them things you wind!" he shouted. "Make one o' them things ya wind!"

So that's what I did. And this is it.

Merry Christmas, Happy Hannukah, Joyeux Nöel, Wassail!

I could have built this thing from scraps in my shop (I had more than would last a lifetime, so the producer had told his secretary) but inspiration sometimes needs to be freshened up. I like to be stirred to action by a box of what most everyone else thinks is useless junk.

I set myself the challenge that I would only use what was in the box and I was to use as much as possible of the stuff.

For a theme I decided on Christmas. It was around the beginning of November and the show was to be aired to woodworkers later in the month.

My idea was that I wanted a dancing doll similar to *Granddad's Night Out*, but I didn't want the depth that was needed for that toy. I wanted to be able to set the toy on a sideboard or mantelpiece. I devised a shallow mechanism and that's what's here. It has it's own peculiar rattle and clank, as you will discover when you make one.

Some of the pieces in the box were pointy, wedge-shaped plywood. They were sort of the shape here. I added the curlicues. The two long strips of pine are what started me thinking about the probable final shape of the piece.

I guess our minds are really boxes of scraps. Leftovers, memories of things good and bad, ends—we make what we can of them; each to each, according to the season and what we need and what we think will work, please others, or help us have a nicer life.

Plan Views of Parts

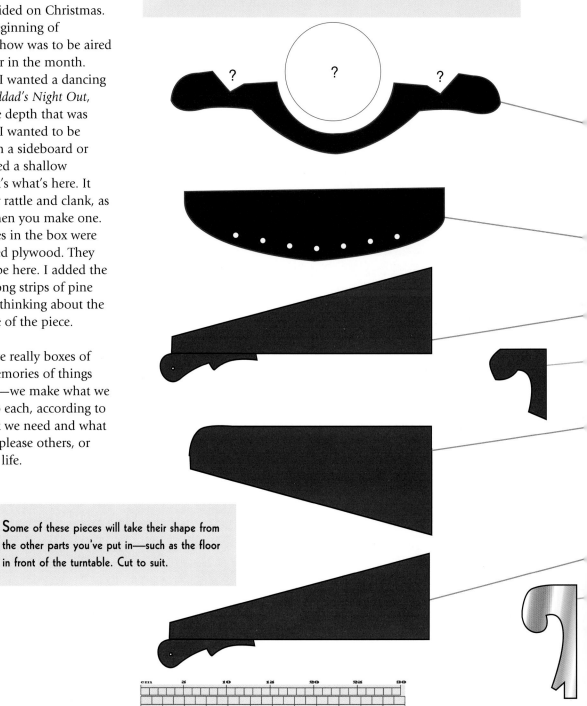

The pieces with the rows of holes were actually a spoon rack (made in Taiwan, I left the label on) that got into the box of scrap while on its way to me. Someone thought that it was the garbage being taken out! So incorporate something of your own stuff that was destined for the garbage.

Some of these pieces will take their shape from the other parts you've put in—such as the floor in front of the turntable. Cut to suit.

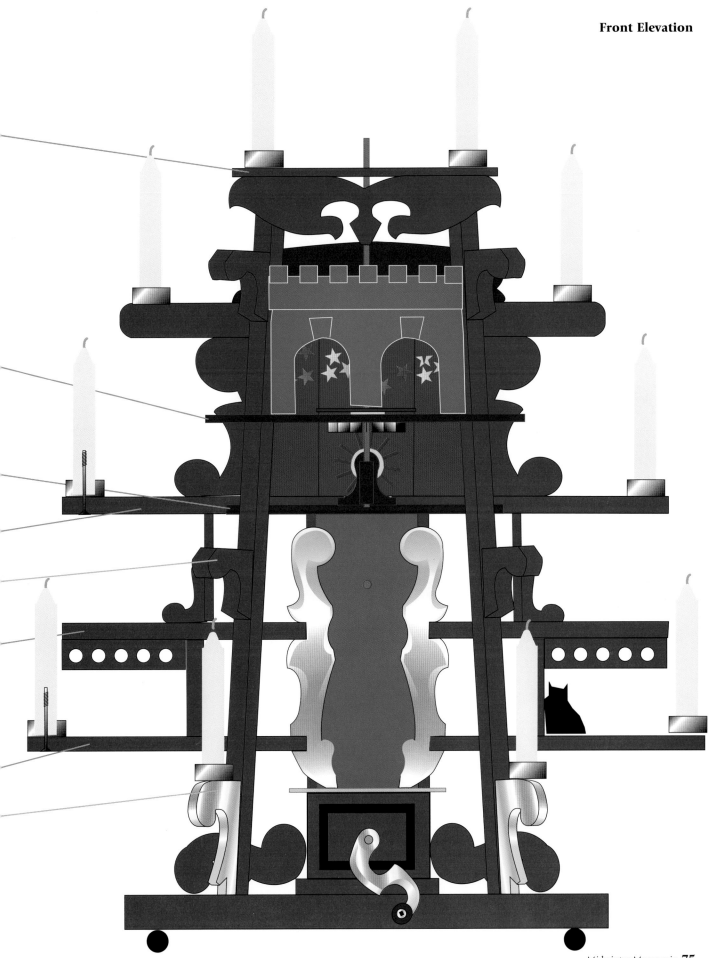

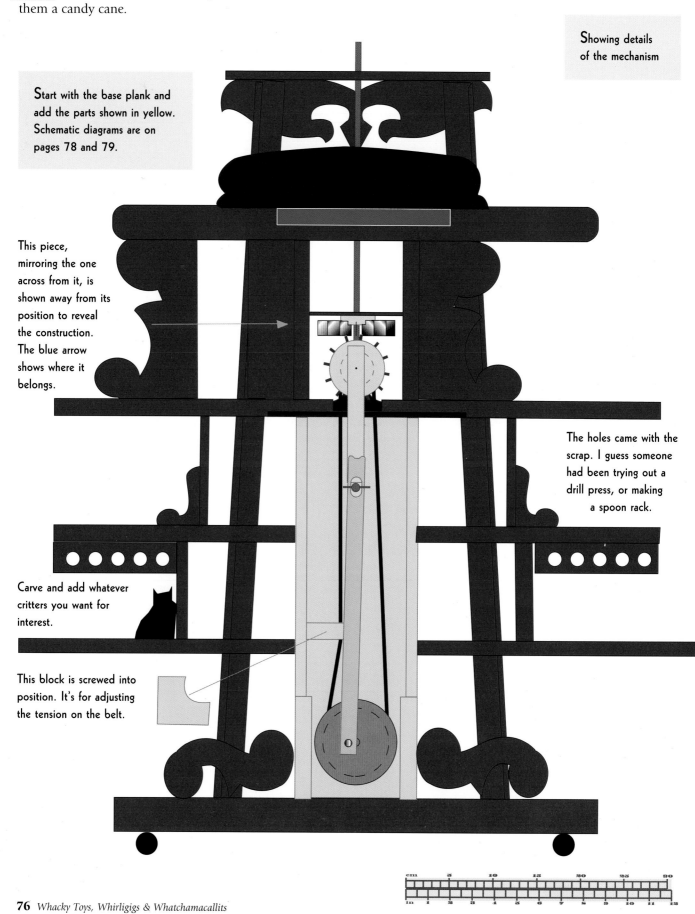

W hen kids come in at Christmas,
I crank for them and then give
them a candy cane.

Showing details
of the mechanism

Start with the base plank and
add the parts shown in yellow.
Schematic diagrams are on
pages 78 and 79.

This piece,
mirroring the one
across from it, is
shown away from its
position to reveal
the construction.
The blue arrow
shows where it
belongs.

The holes came with the
scrap. I guess someone
had been trying out a
drill press, or making
a spoon rack.

Carve and add whatever
critters you want for
interest.

This block is screwed into
position. It's for adjusting
the tension on the belt.

Side Elevation &
Cross Section

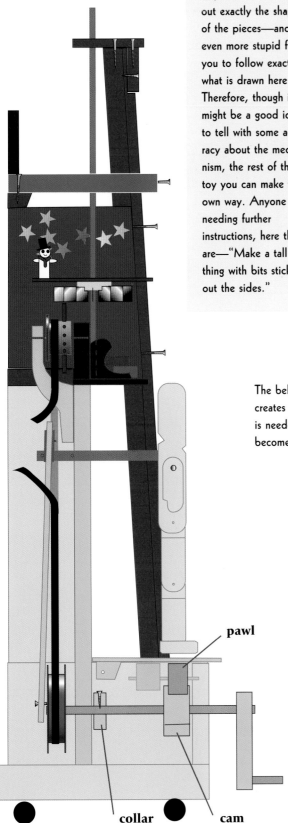

The belt (black) is cut away to show the elastic, which creates a flexible joint for the doll's dowel. This elastic is needed because the doll will otherwise sometimes become jammed by the rising floor.

pawl

collar   cam

The large dancing doll is on a ⅜" dowel. The dowel passes loosely through the backboard. A bamboo skewer through the dowel holds the dowel from coming forward. The rear end of the dowel is moved up and down by a pitman (connecting rod) attached to an offset on a wheel. The dowel passes through a slot in the pitman and is held by a bamboo skewer. An elastic band passes around the dowel and onto both sides of the pitman, holding the dowel into the upper end of the slot. The wheel that drives the pitman is activated by a handle on the front of the toy.

The floor on which the doll dances moves up and down. Under the floor is a cam and a pawl (see the detailed drawings on page 80). On the drive shaft is a collar to keep the shaft in place.

The crank turns a wheel that drives a belt that turns a sprocket. The sprocket engages a sprocket set horizontally and on the vertical drive shaft. This turns the turntable and the universe on top.

Schematic Drawings

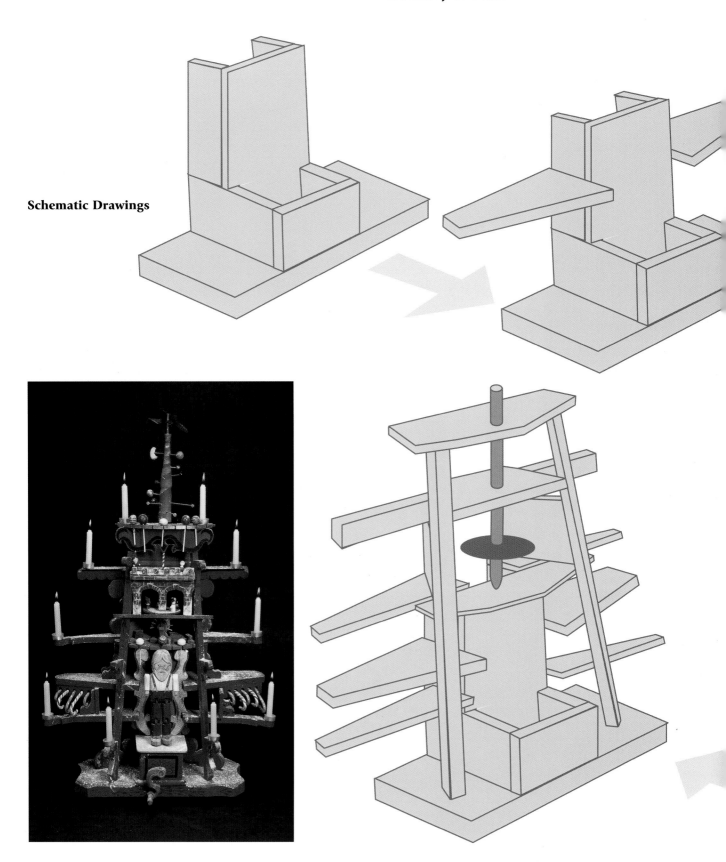

This is basically the way this toy goes together but, as I said, I made it from scraps. So if you've got scraps that'll look or work better . . .

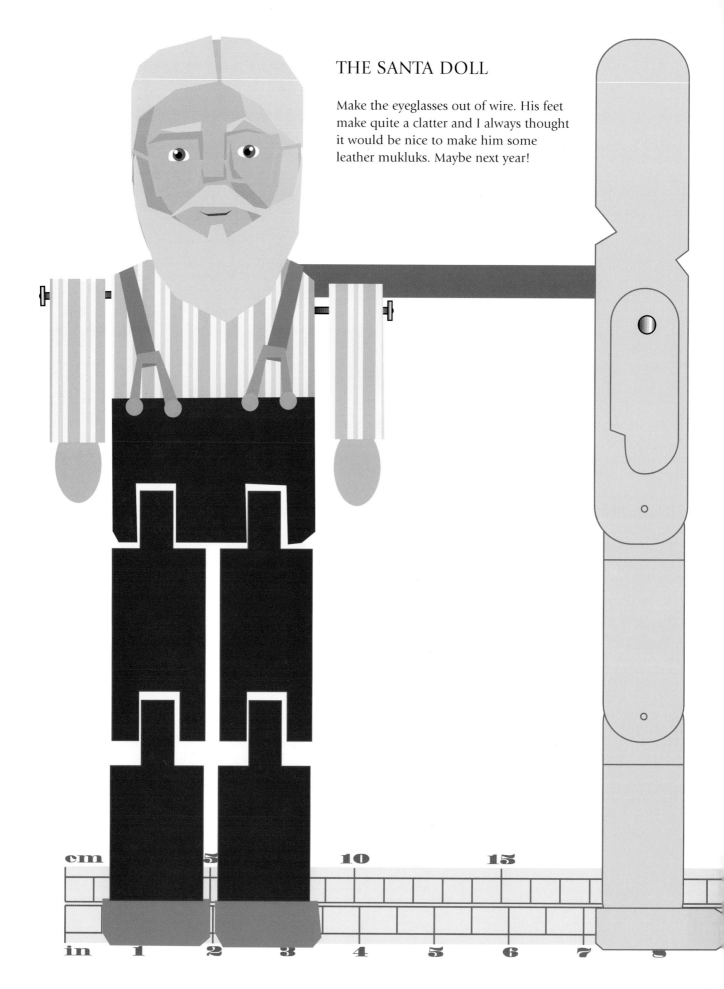

THE SANTA DOLL

Make the eyeglasses out of wire. His feet make quite a clatter and I always thought it would be nice to make him some leather mukluks. Maybe next year!

cm | 5 | 10 | 15

in | 1 | 2 | 3 | 4 | 5 | 6 | 7 | 8

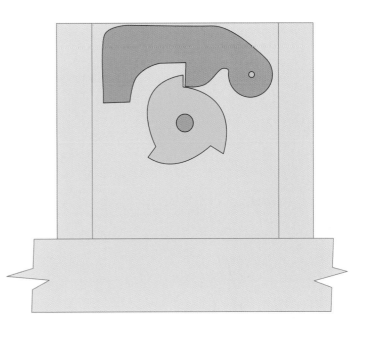

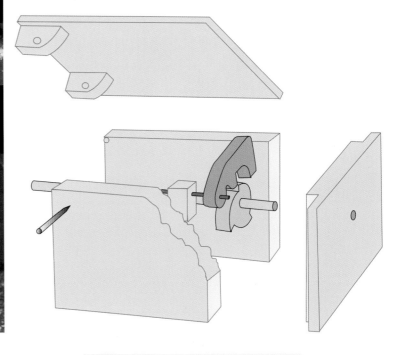

Schematic drawing showing the assembly of the floor to the pawl and cam box.

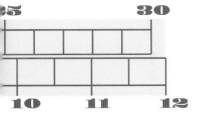

THE UNIVERSE

The universe can be any size you want. This one started out as a lathe demo and, whoops, it got into the scrap box. Make yours square or hex; it doesn't matter. Taper off a piece of pine or use an old piece of chair leg. The systems are bamboo skewers. The planets and stars are beads and jewelry from a flea market. I painted the planets by coating them with shellac and, while they were still tacky, I dipped them in bronzing powders. Great effect!

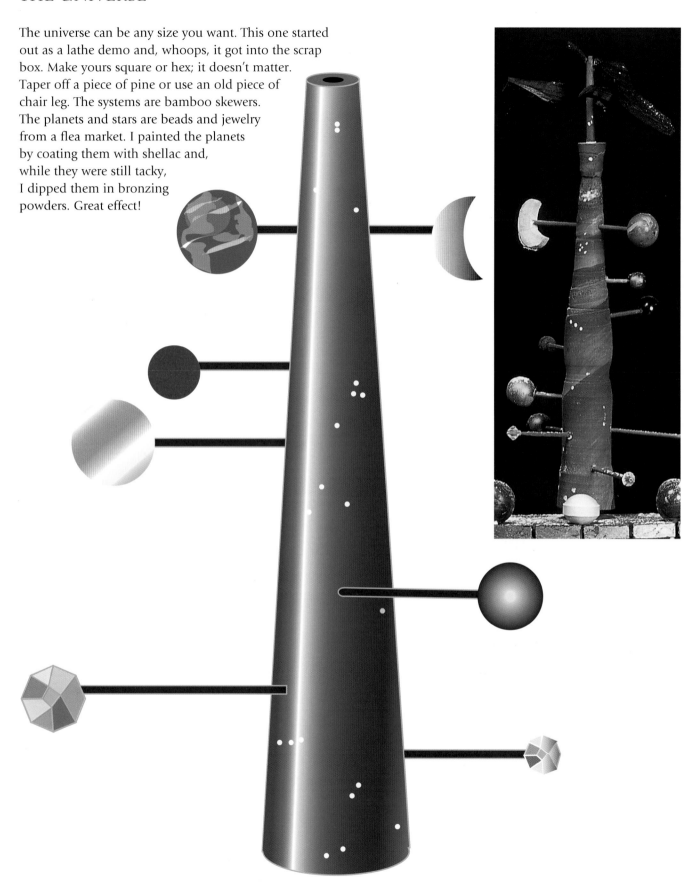

THE RAVENS

In the Norse tradition, "Huginn" and "Muninn" are two ravens that fly around the world every day and then go back to Odin who had given an eye for wisdom and who has been riding with spear in hand his eight-legged horse, meanwhile. Huginn and Muninn tell him what's been going on. Odin's day comes down to us as Woden's day,   or Wednesday.

Make them out of pine scraps for bodies and ⅛" ply for wings.

Maybe you would prefer angels. Do it!

God Says, You Chuze

Nobody makes decisions for us—we make them ourselves. Maybe it seems like someone else has made us decide something but, if we think about it, we realize that we—even when we've been persuaded—do the choosing.

Some folks try to get out of this truth by inventing other truths, such as, "the devil made me do it" or maybe, "God is telling me to do this." The only thing I think any god says is this—"you make up your own mind, you decide, you chuze!"

And I will!

How did I ever get an idea like this, and is it hard to make? After a while with thinking up and working with these machines, a person doesn't even know what is complicated and what is not! Take this one—is it involved or is it simple?

Any task broken down to its parts can be tackled without much ado. I started out trying to decide how to display a series of dolls that I had been working on. A show was coming up, and I'd been asked to show what I was doing of recent times and of my interest.

I laid out the dolls on the bench and was thinking of maybe displaying them like butterflies, on a card with big pins stuck through them, when my eyes lit upon a piece of round wood—a disc of some hard wood that I had recently got from the effects of Joe Gaudaur, who had died a coupla years ago—his daughter Judy had given me a load of stuff from his workshop. Well the dolls and the disc sort of got stuck together in my mind and I started fiddling them around together. Suppose, I thought, these pieces went together; what would happen if, instead of rows of dolls, I had them go around. Then what?

Then what? What if they all went around on a disc like a target. Why? What for? What are they doing going around? Like a target. A target revolving and . . . ?

I looked around and on the shelf there was a Mr. Muscles put aside and now available for something else. What is he doing with these women (all the dolls were female)? I held up the disc and then moved him around—of course he was looking at them—no showing off his muscles—his moving arm was missing—he seemed to be looking—pointing his arm (yet to be made)—yes, pointing at them!

This was enough for me; that was it. Now all I had to do was make the machine that would drive the effect.

Gradually, I made first this piece and then that as I needed it. Something to hold the disc; something to enable it to revolve. A base plank for him to stand on. I found a compost sifter that I had once made and then used for a while as an end table and then put back in the shop (probably to complete as a compost sifter).

On the page to the left we see that *God Says, You Chuze* is a stand with a frame above it. On the frame stands a pointing guy. At one end of the frame is a board with a pulley on one side; and a disc on which are fixed four different dolls. They don't have to be different—if you make them all the same, then you will have a different idea than the one that I have decided to use. Come to think of it instead of dolls one could put plates of spaghetti, pizza, beans, ice cream—you chuze!

The arrow shows that the rotary motion of the crankshaft needs to be translated into an oscillating motion to move the arm up and down. The mechanism for turning the belt that turns the dolls and for translating this motion to move the Chuzer's arm is shown in more detail on pages 88 to 91 and on pages 94 to 95.

The middle frame for this machine is, as I say, the remains of a compost sifter; but don't let that put you off—what it is really is an upside down U-shaped 2 X 6 plank. The plank is made U shaped by cutting it into three pieces and then dovetailing them together.

The dovetails are quite large and are not mandatory; if you would prefer them joined in some other way, go ahead with your idea. There is a lot of pressure put on the toy, so make it solid whatever you do.

To join the middle frame to the base, use hanger bolts. A hanger bolt is part wood screw and part machine bolt. Hanger bolts are easily obtainable at the local store when you know what to ask for. They come in different sizes; ¼ inch is a good general size to keep around.

To put in a hanger bolt:

Drill the hole as you would for any regular wood screw.

Wind a nut onto the bolt end until it won't go any more. Don't tighten it down, just thumb pressure is good.

Put the screw end in the hole, turn the hanger bolt in with your hand, and then snug up with a wrench.

You now have a bolt end sticking out which can be put into the hole provided, just as if you were using an ordinary bolt.

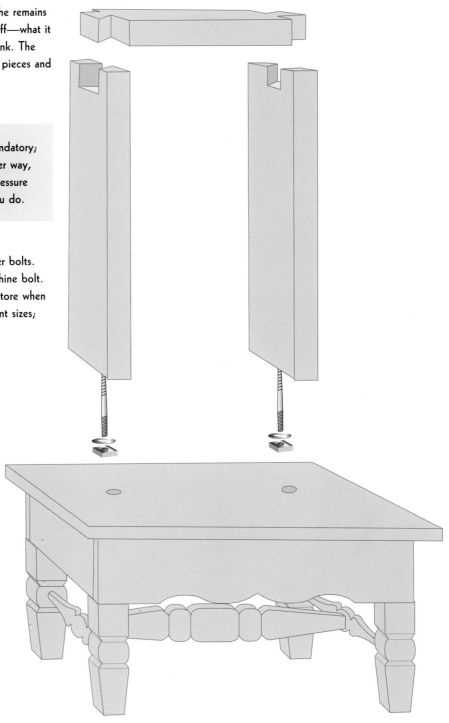

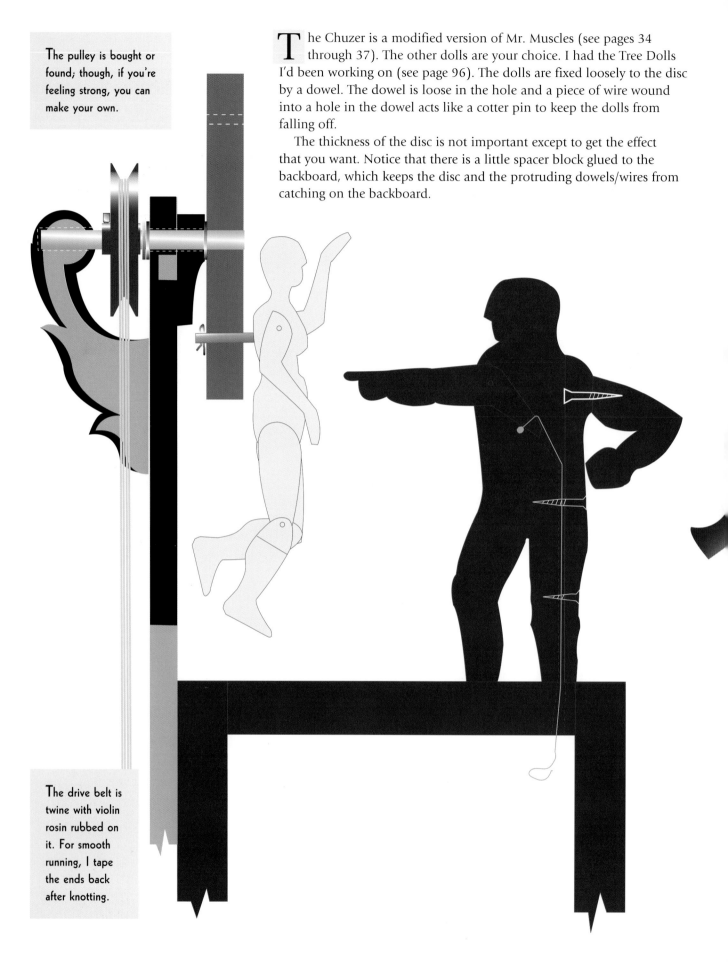

The pulley is bought or found; though, if you're feeling strong, you can make your own.

The Chuzer is a modified version of Mr. Muscles (see pages 34 through 37). The other dolls are your choice. I had the Tree Dolls I'd been working on (see page 96). The dolls are fixed loosely to the disc by a dowel. The dowel is loose in the hole and a piece of wire wound into a hole in the dowel acts like a cotter pin to keep the dolls from falling off.

The thickness of the disc is not important except to get the effect that you want. Notice that there is a little spacer block glued to the backboard, which keeps the disc and the protruding dowels/wires from catching on the backboard.

The drive belt is twine with violin rosin rubbed on it. For smooth running, I tape the ends back after knotting.

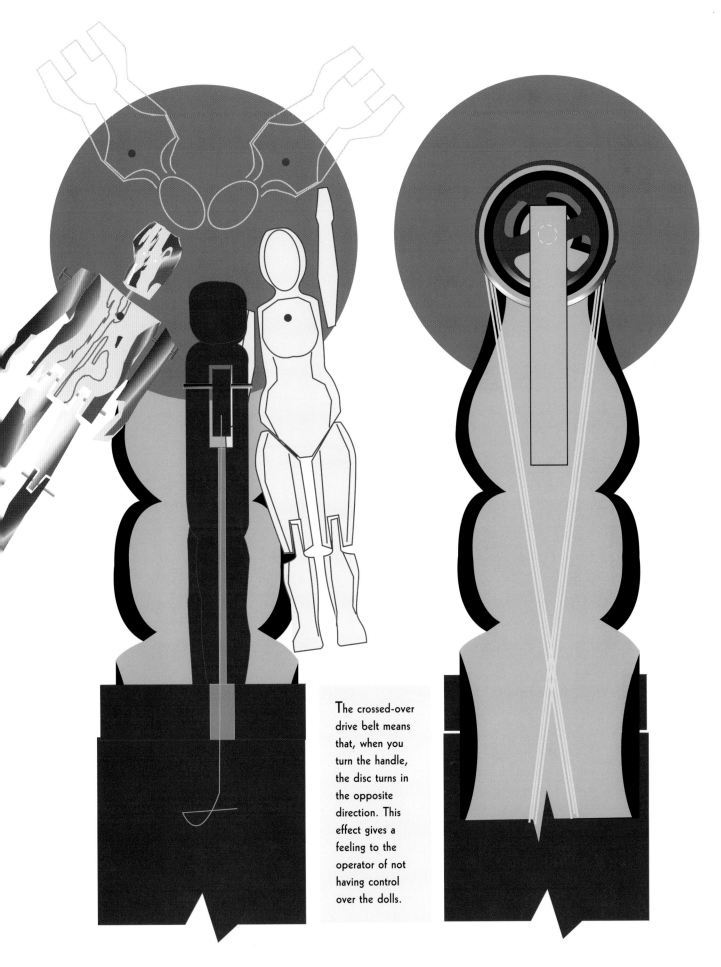

The crossed-over drive belt means that, when you turn the handle, the disc turns in the opposite direction. This effect gives a feeling to the operator of not having control over the dolls.

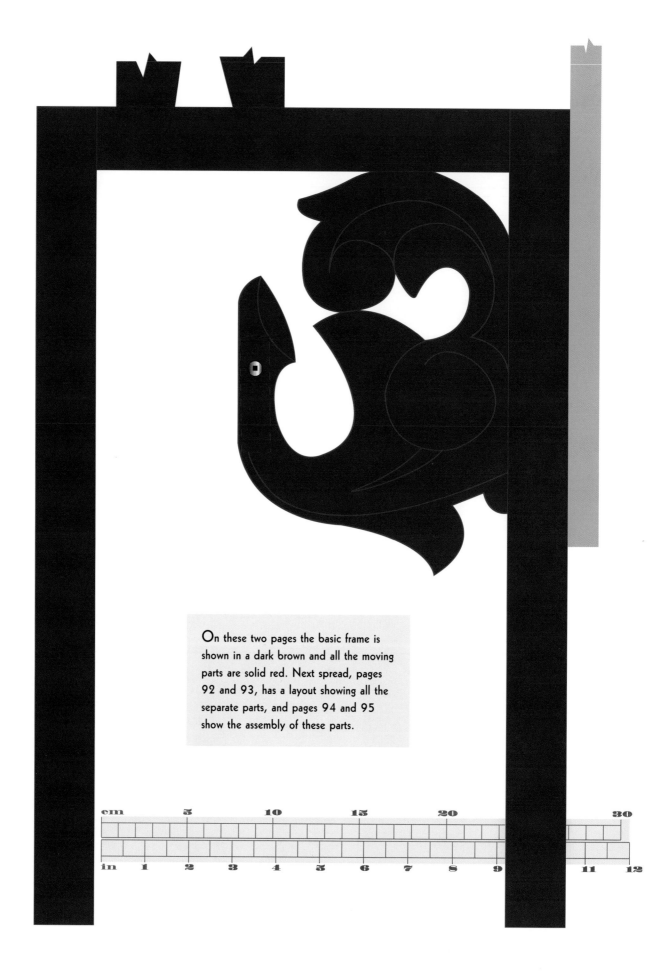

On these two pages the basic frame is shown in a dark brown and all the moving parts are solid red. Next spread, pages 92 and 93, has a layout showing all the separate parts, and pages 94 and 95 show the assembly of these parts.

I have not shown the carved parts of the frame here for the same reason that I have not shown the moving parts on the opposite page—clarity. See the assembly steps on pages 94 and 95 to see more of how the mechanism works.

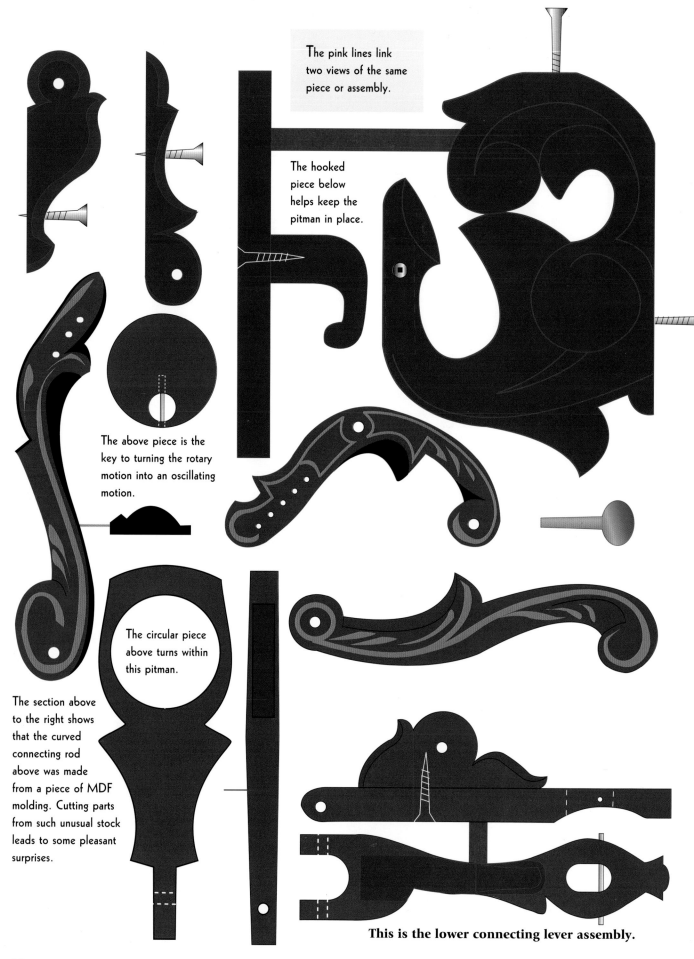

The pink lines link two views of the same piece or assembly.

The hooked piece below helps keep the pitman in place.

The above piece is the key to turning the rotary motion into an oscillating motion.

The circular piece above turns within this pitman.

The section above to the right shows that the curved connecting rod above was made from a piece of MDF molding. Cutting parts from such unusual stock leads to some pleasant surprises.

This is the lower connecting lever assembly.

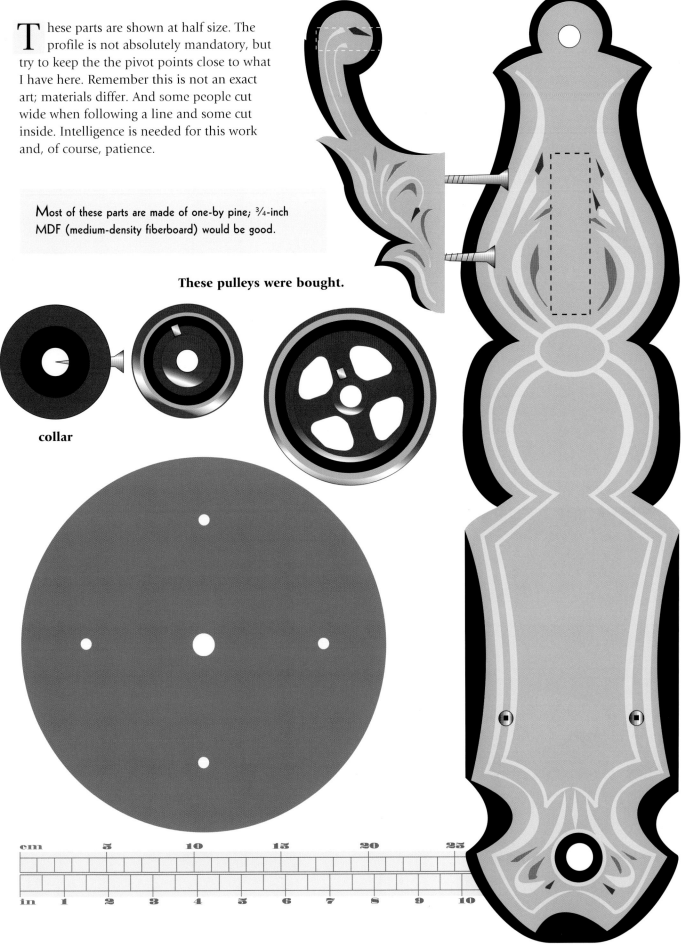

T hese parts are shown at half size. The profile is not absolutely mandatory, but try to keep the the pivot points close to what I have here. Remember this is not an exact art; materials differ. And some people cut wide when following a line and some cut inside. Intelligence is needed for this work and, of course, patience.

Most of these parts are made of one-by pine; ¾-inch MDF (medium-density fiberboard) would be good.

These pulleys were bought.

collar

cm   5   10   15   20   25

in   1   2   3   4   5   6   7   8   9   10

SEQUENCE OF ASSEMBLY

Assemble the parts in the order shown in the diagrams at the bottom of this page spread.

The piece shown in green is the lower connecting lever. The arm shown in pink is the upper support, which rides up and down on the pitman, helping keep it in place (along with the hooked piece shown by the gray square outlined in white).

The piece shown in blue moves the string for the arm and is linked to the curved connecting rod (shown in red) that links the movement to the lower (green) connecting lever.

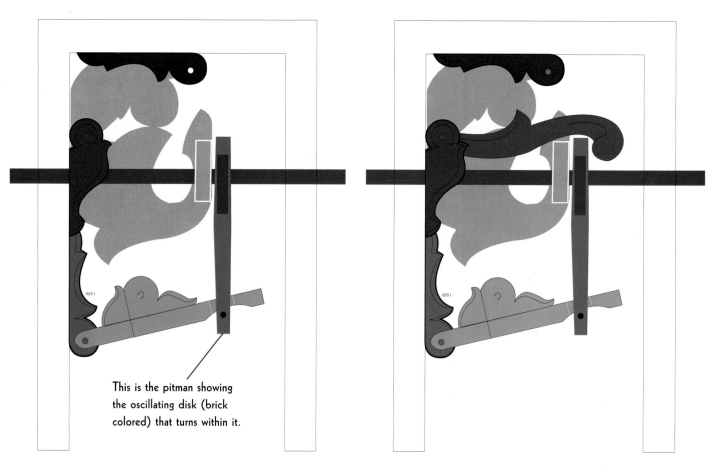

This is the pitman showing the oscillating disk (brick colored) that turns within it.

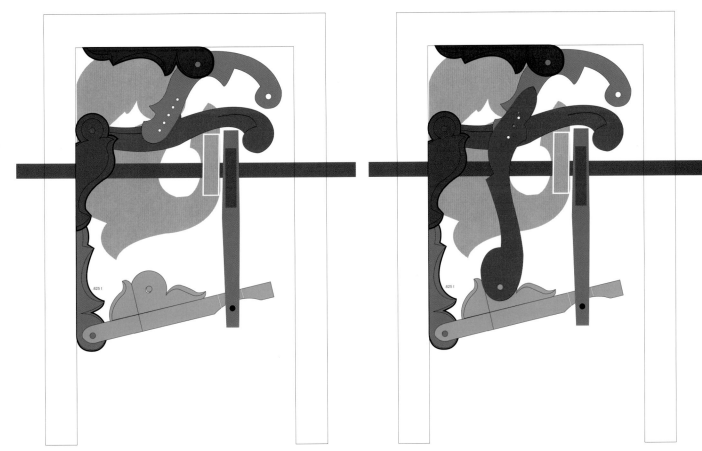

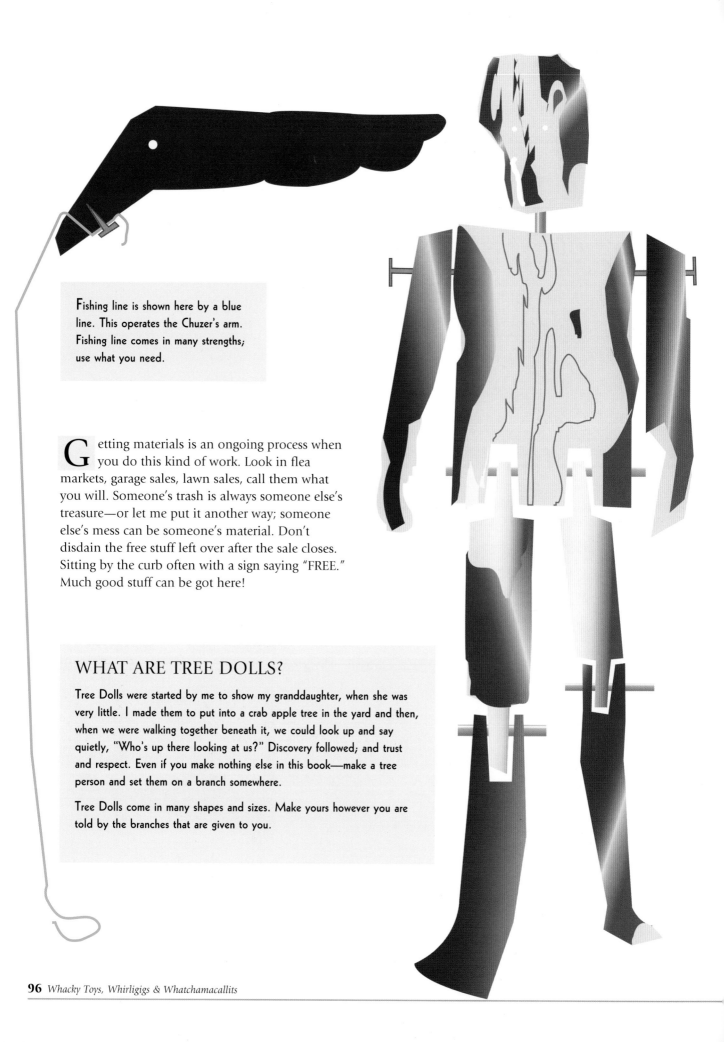

Fishing line is shown here by a blue line. This operates the Chuzer's arm. Fishing line comes in many strengths; use what you need.

Getting materials is an ongoing process when you do this kind of work. Look in flea markets, garage sales, lawn sales, call them what you will. Someone's trash is always someone else's treasure—or let me put it another way; someone else's mess can be someone's material. Don't disdain the free stuff left over after the sale closes. Sitting by the curb often with a sign saying "FREE." Much good stuff can be got here!

WHAT ARE TREE DOLLS?

Tree Dolls were started by me to show my granddaughter, when she was very little. I made them to put into a crab apple tree in the yard and then, when we were walking together beneath it, we could look up and say quietly, "Who's up there looking at us?" Discovery followed; and trust and respect. Even if you make nothing else in this book—make a tree person and set them on a branch somewhere.

Tree Dolls come in many shapes and sizes. Make yours however you are told by the branches that are given to you.

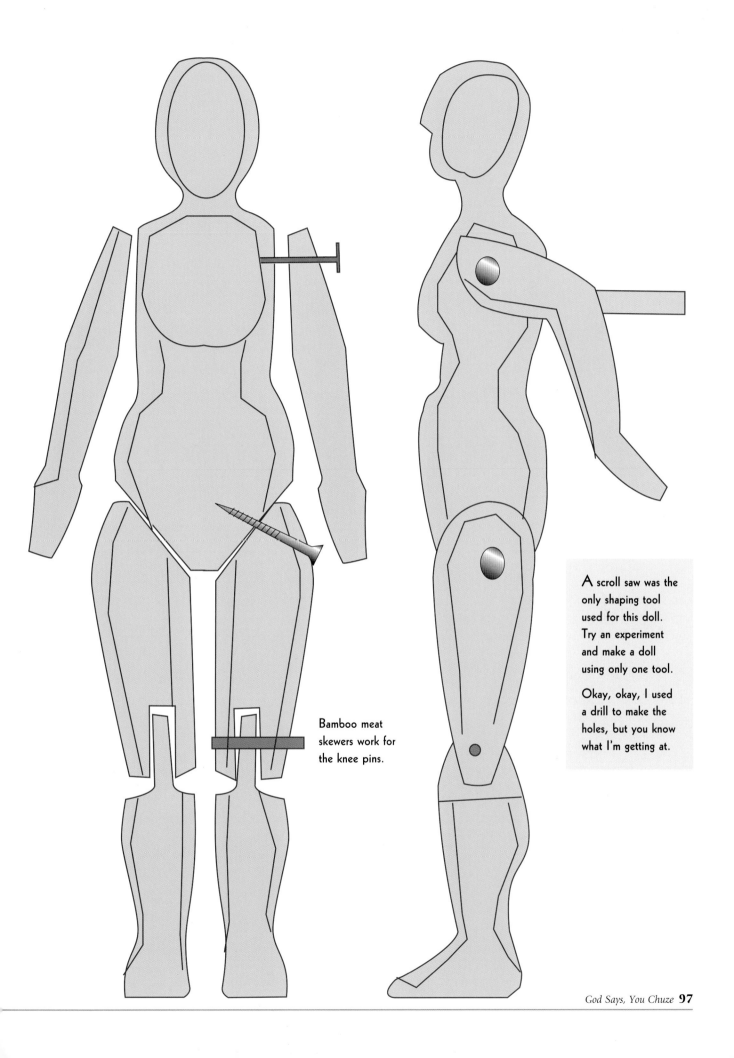

Bamboo meat skewers work for the knee pins.

A scroll saw was the only shaping tool used for this doll. Try an experiment and make a doll using only one tool.

Okay, okay, I used a drill to make the holes, but you know what I'm getting at.

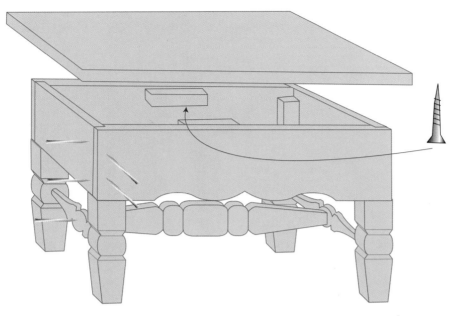

Note in this schematic drawing that short blocks attached to the long side pieces allow the top to be attached with screws.

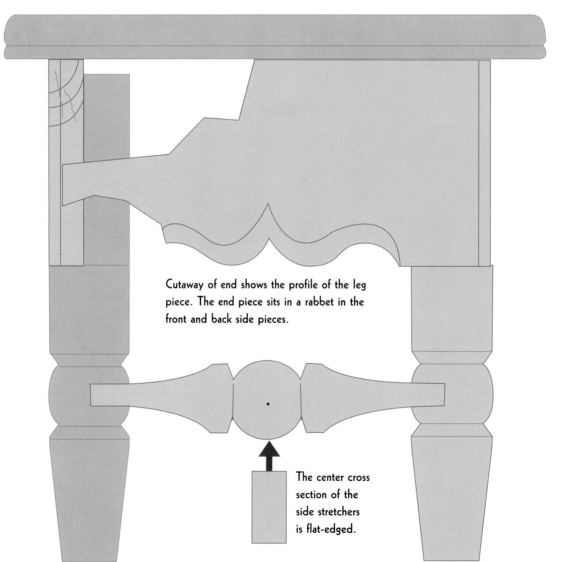

Cutaway of end shows the profile of the leg piece. The end piece sits in a rabbet in the front and back side pieces.

The center cross section of the side stretchers is flat-edged.

T he stand is really just a simple table or stool. You could make this just by itself for a nice project and feel good about it!

Have fun experimenting with some decorative painting, such as the design I have used.

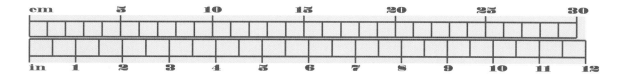

The long stretcher has a circular cross section throughout.

The In-Flight Movie, a Whirligig & Crank Toy

One day I bumped into Gord, the guy from next door who spends most of his time in his basement prospecting for gold—from old computers.

"Haven't seen you around for a while," says Gord.

"Been in my basement making a TV," I reply.

"A TV?" says Gord, puzzled. "I thought you worked in wood."

"I do," I says. "I do, but it's only for looking at."

"Oh right!" says Gord, satisfied and walks on his way with a settled mind.

I still wonder what else TVs are used for. This is what I was making.

The TV idea came to me on a plane as I was eating chicken, high above the Atlantic. Chickens are birds, I thought, yet I am the one in the air. Strange mood, not helped by the film "Forrest Gump" playing on the screen(s) in front of me.

Despite the special effects in the movie, the screens could well have been set in a bar in the early days of color TV—bright blue and orange! Someone on the other side of the football-field-sized cabin asked whether something could be done to fix the color; unsuccessful attempts were made by uniformed staff. They just shrugged—eat and enjoy the in-flight movie.

Here we were, miles up in the sky, trusting the operators to keep us there with modern technology and they couldn't tune the TV! As I am thinking this the headphones interrupt.

"This is your captain speaking—We are flying at blah, blah, blah . . . and expect to arrive blah, blah, and so on . . . " And we were supposed to believe that someone was actually saying this to us right now—I thought maybe it could have been a tape loaded on-board with the chicken dinners. I mention this to the person that I will never see again, or even know if I do see again—the stranger in the seat beside me. I get the "I-know-you-are-talking-to-me-but" smile and nod.

I help myself to another glass of wine from a passing attendant. Swigging it down in a single gulp, I realize it's cola—warm cola!

With a regular whirligig, the vane turns the propeller into the wind. Because of this the toy is seen from many angles. I wanted a whirligig that would always be facing the same way—then I could watch it, no problem, while sitting in an armchair looking out the window in my front room.

I found a drawing in an old book showing a propeller that revolves without being turned into the wind. The device is called a pantanenome, the principles of which I've decribed on page 9. Read that explanation and follow the instructions on pages 106 and 107 to make the one for this toy.

After building this toy, I grew impatient, waiting for the wind to blow, and converted it to manual power. I left the pantanenome on it though 'cause it looks good, and maybe the wind will blow one day!

**Schematic Drawing
Showing the
Pantanenome &
Crank Mechanism**

YOUR NAME HERE

T here are very few (if any) critical measurements in this toy. The scale will give you what you need to step off with dividers.

Back, Front, and Side Elevations with Details of the Mechanism

As usual most of the wood is one-by pine—easy to get, easy to work!

The schematic assembly sequence is shown on pages 108 and 109.

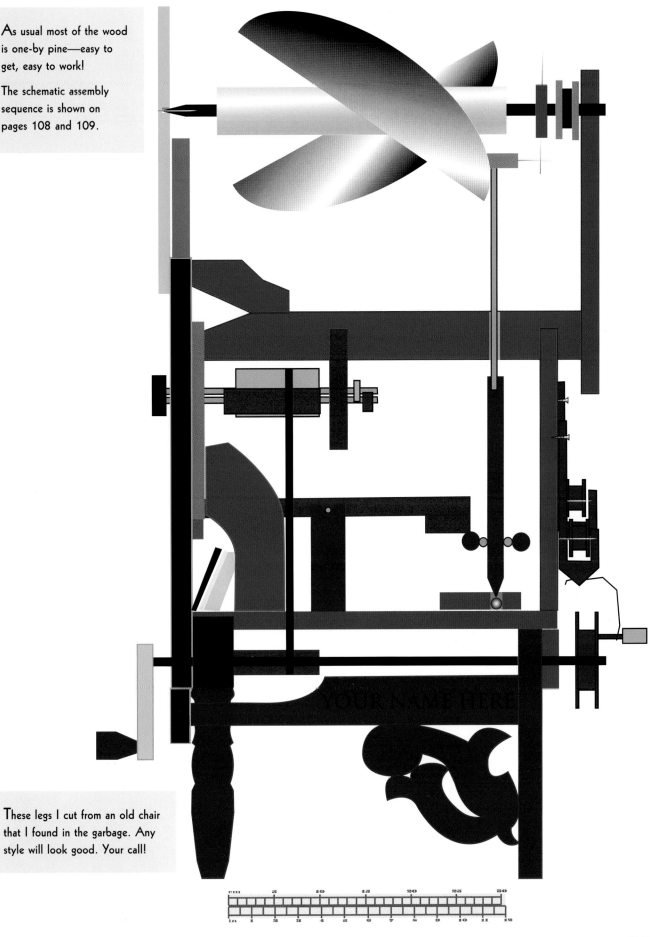

YOUR NAME HERE

These legs I cut from an old chair that I found in the garbage. Any style will look good. Your call!

MAKING THE PANTANENOME

Make the pantanenome from a piece of plastic plumbing pipe. Two cuts are sawn in from opposite sides at 45° to the pipe sides.

Inside the pipe are two discs (I was lucky and found some jar caps that fit exactly—you may have something around that would do, too). At the end of the shaft (shown here in black) are the cog (blue) and pulley (red) for transferring power from the winder. The front end of the shaft is pointed and has a nail that bears in a small hole in the "lightning flash" on the front.

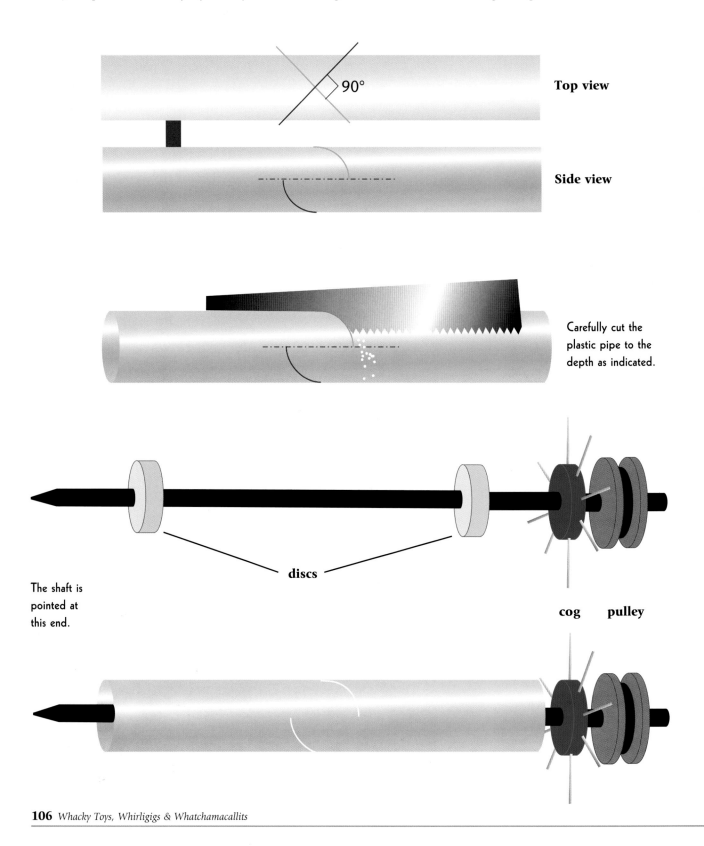

Top view

90°

Side view

Carefully cut the plastic pipe to the depth as indicated.

discs

The shaft is pointed at this end.

cog   pulley

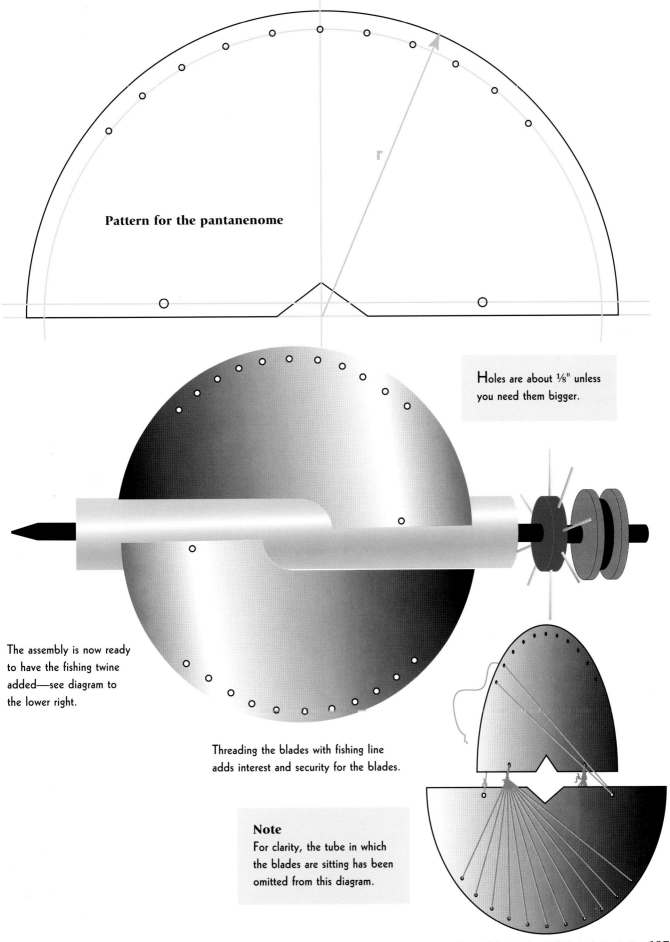

Pattern for the pantanenome

r

Holes are about ⅛" unless you need them bigger.

The assembly is now ready to have the fishing twine added—see diagram to the lower right.

Threading the blades with fishing line adds interest and security for the blades.

Note
For clarity, the tube in which the blades are sitting has been omitted from this diagram.

ASSEMBLY SEQUENCE & DETAILS OF MECHANISM

Take your time building these machines. If you run into difficulties, think about what you want and be calm.

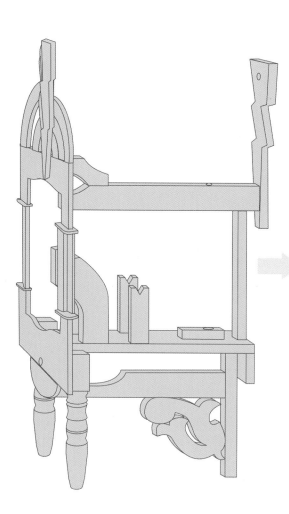

Schematic Drawings

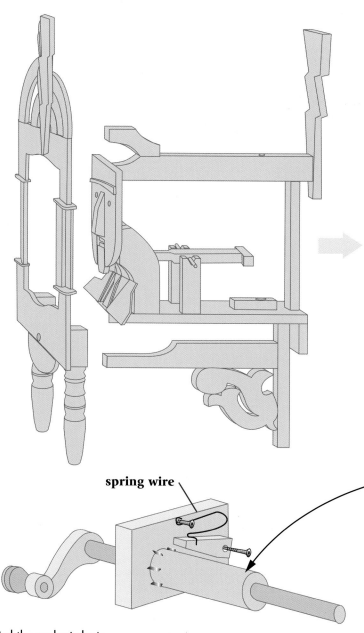

spring wire

These diagrams should help you assemble the parts but let me say this—

Cut the parts as you go; don't cut a whole bunch and try to assemble them or you will be frustrated!

Behind the crank winder is a ratchet. This is made by inserting strips of metal into saw cuts. A piece of music or spring wire keeps the wooden pawl in place. This ratchet makes an interesting clicking sound. If you want it to be left-handed, put the pawl on the opposite side of the shaft.

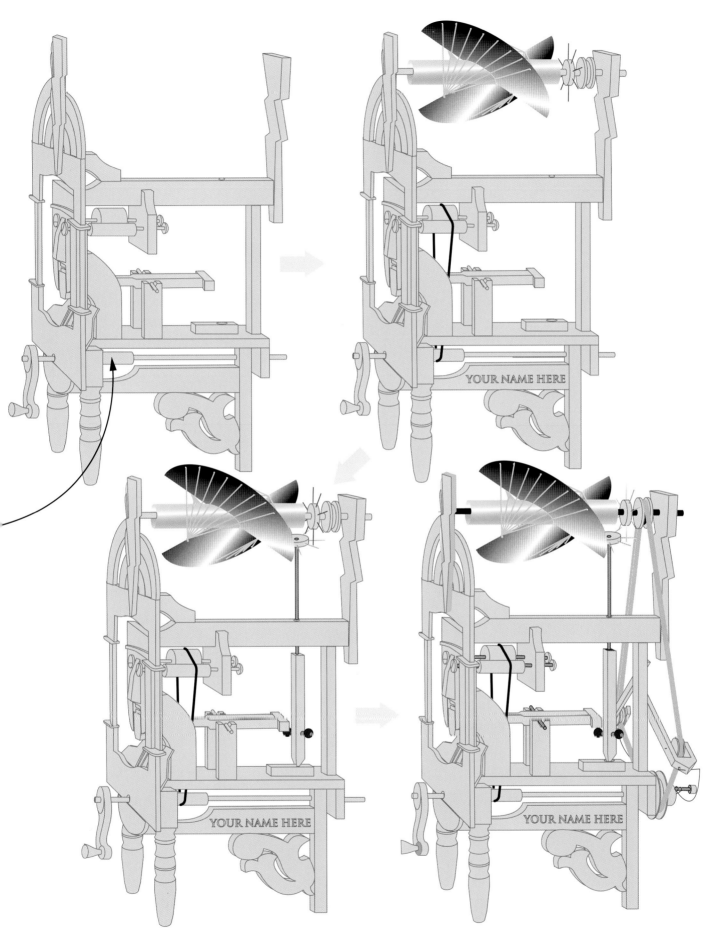

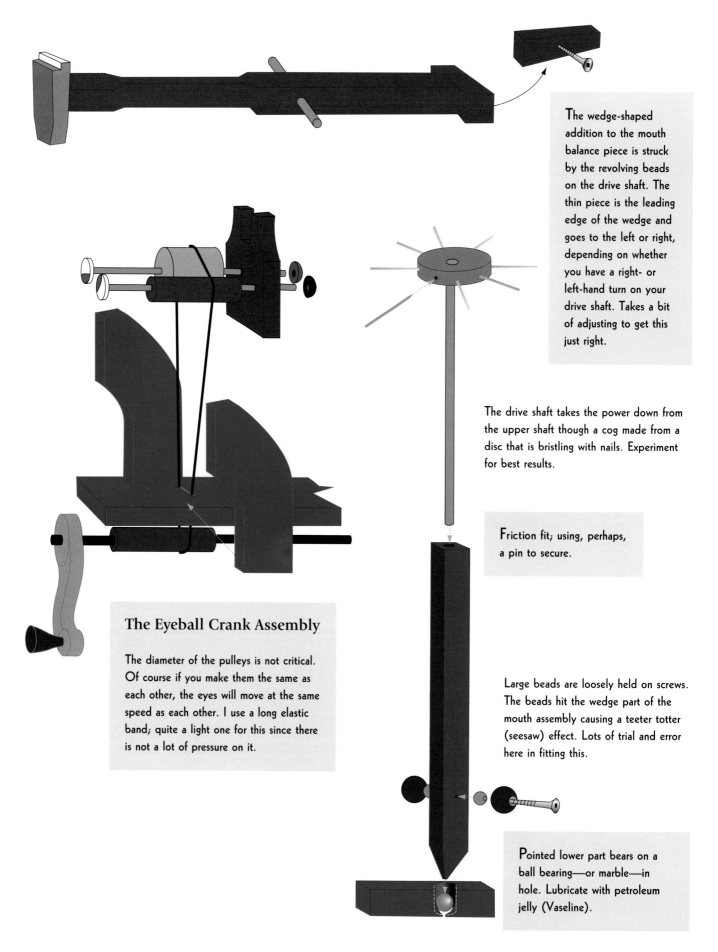

The wedge-shaped addition to the mouth balance piece is struck by the revolving beads on the drive shaft. The thin piece is the leading edge of the wedge and goes to the left or right, depending on whether you have a right- or left-hand turn on your drive shaft. Takes a bit of adjusting to get this just right.

The drive shaft takes the power down from the upper shaft though a cog made from a disc that is bristling with nails. Experiment for best results.

Friction fit; using, perhaps, a pin to secure.

The Eyeball Crank Assembly

The diameter of the pulleys is not critical. Of course if you make them the same as each other, the eyes will move at the same speed as each other. I use a long elastic band; quite a light one for this since there is not a lot of pressure on it.

Large beads are loosely held on screws. The beads hit the wedge part of the mouth assembly causing a teeter totter (seesaw) effect. Lots of trial and error here in fitting this.

Pointed lower part bears on a ball bearing—or marble—in hole. Lubricate with petroleum jelly (Vaseline).

DETAILS OF THE MECHANISM

Drive is transmitted through the handle to the back of the machine. The large pulley (disc of ¾"-thick wood faced with a disc of ⅛" ply on each side) carries three strands of twine over to two smaller pulleys that are each housed in a J-shaped bracket.

The J brackets and pulleys are activated themselves by lengths of music or spring wire attached to a crank on the large pulley.

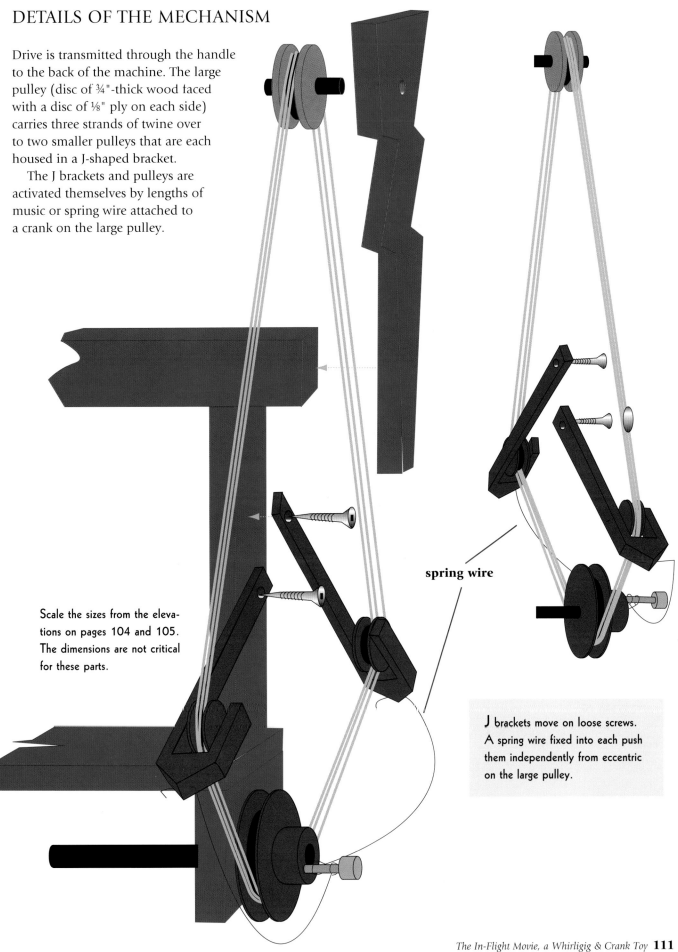

spring wire

Scale the sizes from the elevations on pages 104 and 105. The dimensions are not critical for these parts.

J brackets move on loose screws. A spring wire fixed into each push them independently from eccentric on the large pulley.

Industrious Revolutions, a Credit Card Recycling Machine

*W*hen I showed her a drawing of this machine, the lady who runs the hobby shop on Danforth Avenue in Toronto where I was buying some brass wire said, "This will never sell!" She emigrated from Germany and has a way with words. "It will never sell because the devil is taller than the angel. People do not like that! The angel must be taller than the devil if it is to sell!"

Which one is the angel? Things are not always what they seem at first glance. Why is the tiger wearing red cowboy boots? Is the one in the white shirt defending the dark satanic mills (seen here in pink)? Help yourself to anything you see here but don't take things for granted.

Brass wire, cat food tins, wood, and steel screws make up most of this mysterious machine. And why does the cog wheel at the back have teeth made from pieces of credit card?

H ave fun when you work at these toys. Pretend all you want to pretend. Fake it and make it! I imagined this toy to be the last remaining specimen from some early nineteenth century patent office. Then I imagined that someone found it in the 1960s and so I put the swing tag on it. The tag says, "Industrious Revolutions, circa 1996, Maker Unknown, Prob[ably]—FROST R."

Ideas for toys are everywhere. When I saw the picture below by Thomas Bewick, I knew that I had to make a toy of it.

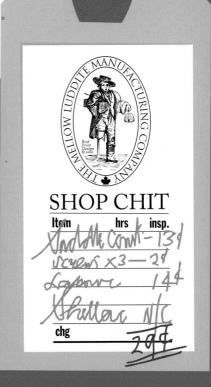

SHOP CHIT

Item	hrs	insp.

chg

INDUSTRIOUS REVOLUTIONS

I	3	5	7	9	II

ONE IMPERIAL FOOT

R . F R O S T H O C F E C I T

Of course, I didn't start out with a blueprint. I'm having fun pretending again.

When, one time, this toy was on exhibition and needed a little adjusting because it was being wound more than usual, I put on the "Shop Chit" as if I had done it years ago. Time tripping is fun to do, costs nothing and mystifies folks.

Some people pretend to get perplexed by such things but let's face it—if you don't want to have to see yourself looking funny, then don't go into the hall of mirrors!

HOC FECIT is latin for "this made." We would say "made this." So R. FROST HOC FECIT means "R. Frost made this."

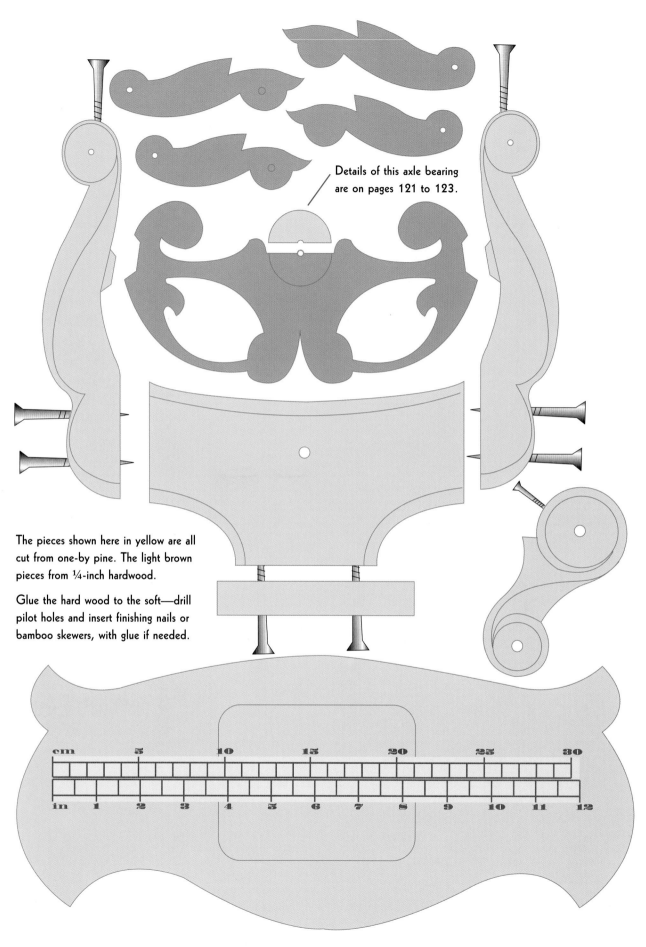

Details of this axle bearing
are on pages 121 to 123.

The pieces shown here in yellow are all
cut from one-by pine. The light brown
pieces from ¼-inch hardwood.

Glue the hard wood to the soft—drill
pilot holes and insert finishing nails or
bamboo skewers, with glue if needed.

cm   5   10   15   20   25   30

in   1   2   3   4   5   6   7   8   9   10   11   12

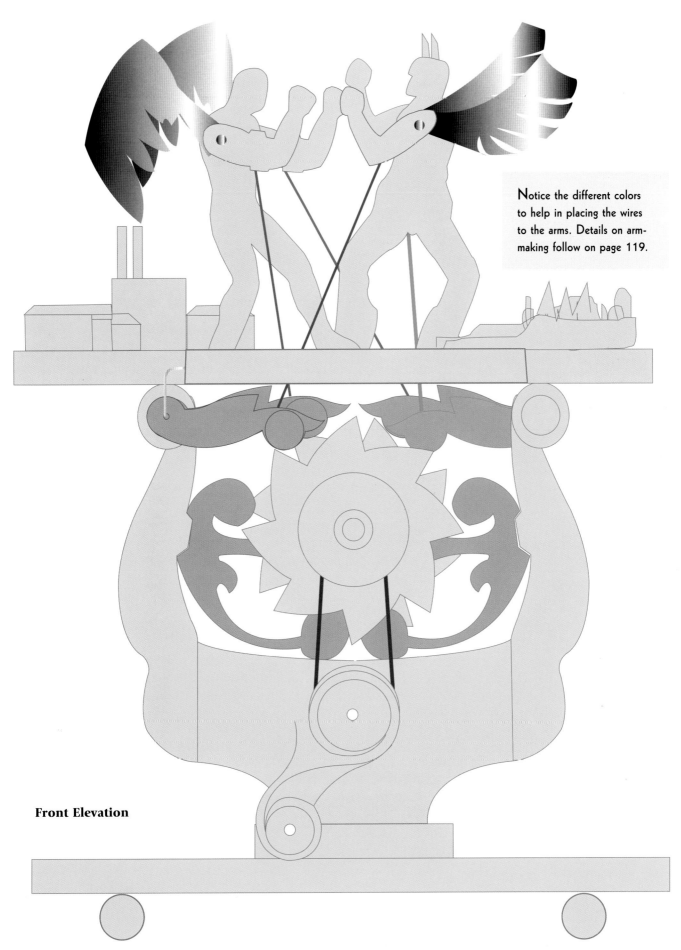

Notice the different colors to help in placing the wires to the arms. Details on arm-making follow on page 119.

Front Elevation

T his shows the placement of the feet and the approximate position of the holes for the wires. Notice that I said approximate!

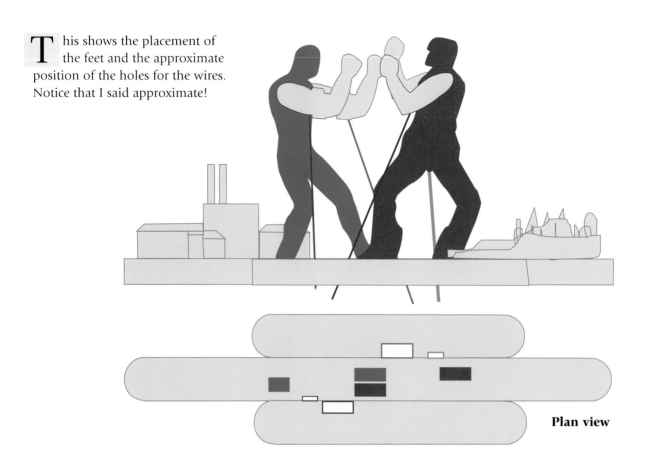

Plan view

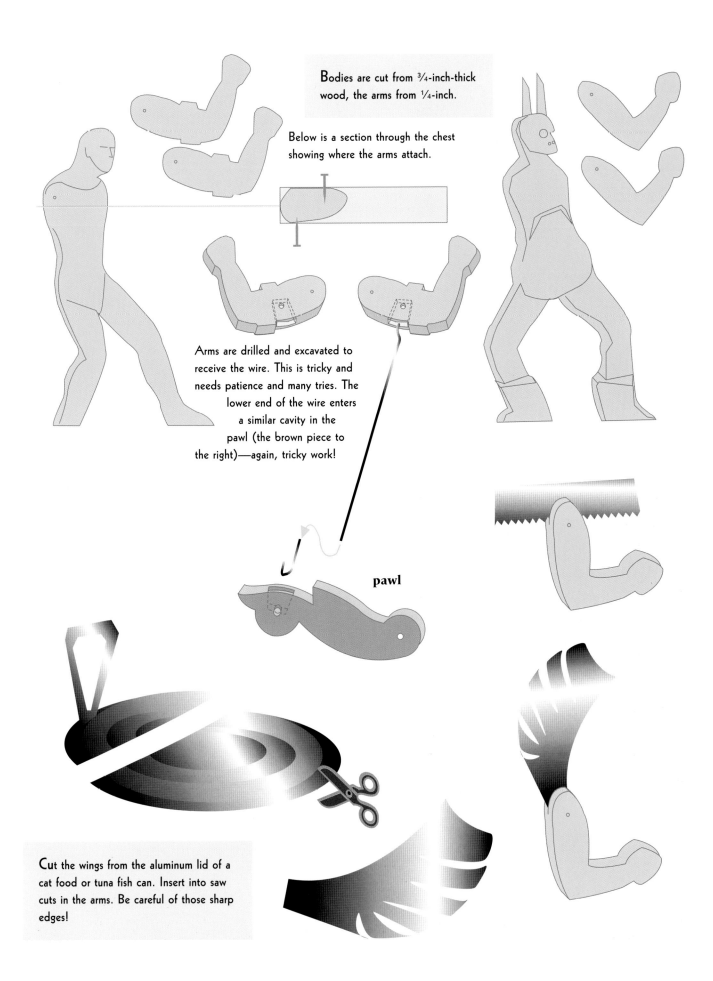

Bodies are cut from ¾-inch-thick wood, the arms from ¼-inch.

Below is a section through the chest showing where the arms attach.

Arms are drilled and excavated to receive the wire. This is tricky and needs patience and many tries. The lower end of the wire enters a similar cavity in the pawl (the brown piece to the right)—again, tricky work!

pawl

Cut the wings from the aluminum lid of a cat food or tuna fish can. Insert into saw cuts in the arms. Be careful of those sharp edges!

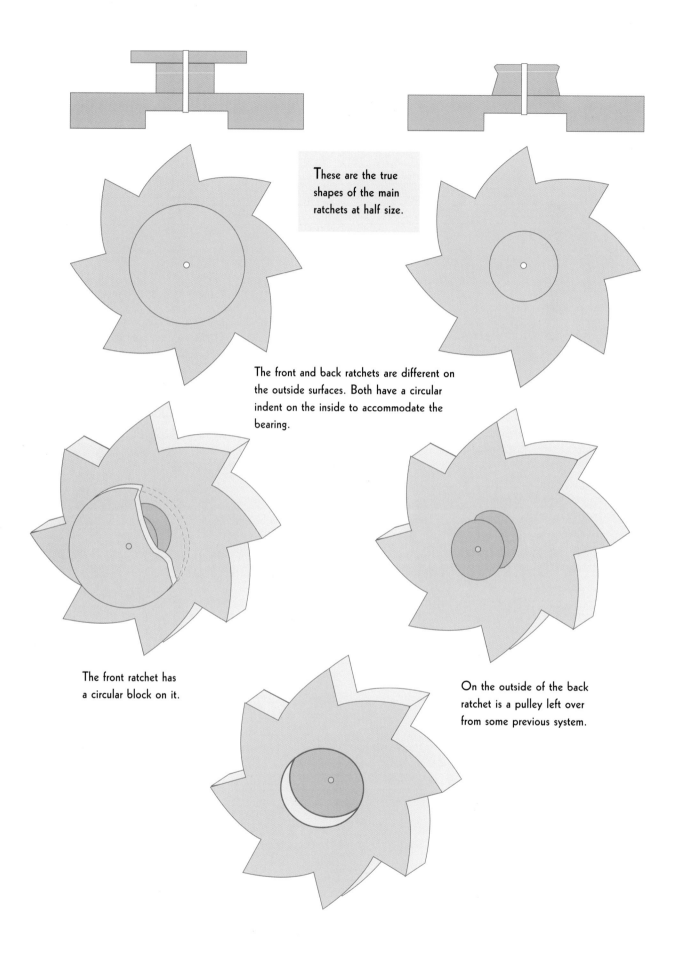

These are the true shapes of the main ratchets at half size.

The front and back ratchets are different on the outside surfaces. Both have a circular indent on the inside to accommodate the bearing.

The front ratchet has a circular block on it.

On the outside of the back ratchet is a pulley left over from some previous system.

MAKING AN AXLE BEARING

Getting holes to line up and be square is one of the principal frustrations in making these toys, particularly if you don't have a drill press. However the ingenious maker and designer can always come up with cheap ways to solve problems.

On this toy there are two ways used to get an axle hole to be accurate without using a drill press.

The example shown at the right is for the rachet axle bearing. It is a tube in a saw cut with the saddle glued on top of it.

The example for the main drive rod can be seen in the photograph below and in the back angled view on page 123. It is a saddle made of a strip of metal bent over the spindle and fixed with screws or nails.

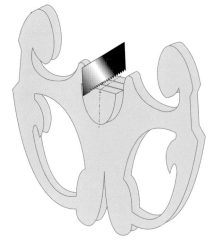

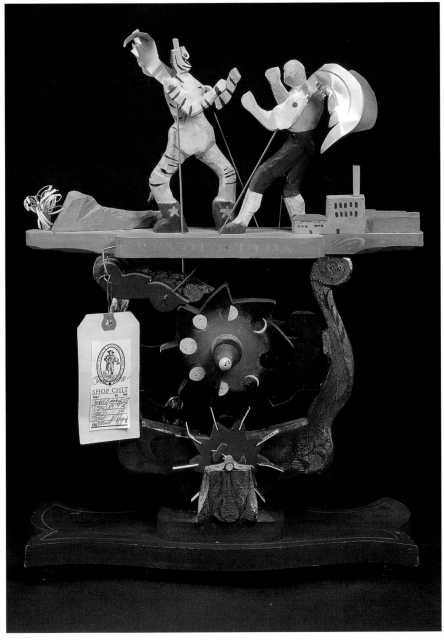

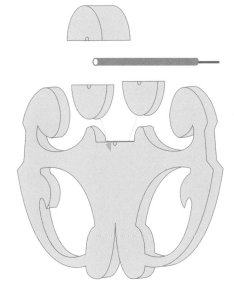

CRANK MECHANISM ASSEMBLY

The ratchet on front and back turn in opposite directions. They are on a common axle. The axle is made of a narrow tube with a wire running through it. The wire extends out of each end and is twisted to keep some decorative beads in place, which in turn hold the ratchet and prevent them from falling off the axle.

The front assembly is driven by a belt (I used a leather scrap) running around a spool (I wrapped felt around the spool to give it a little more friction).

The main drive axle goes through and turns a sprocket armed with slices of credit cards, as shown in the back view on the opposite page.

Schematic Drawings

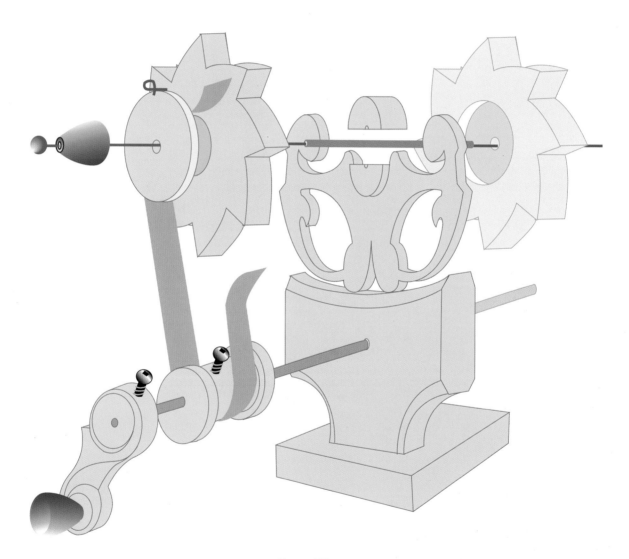

Front View

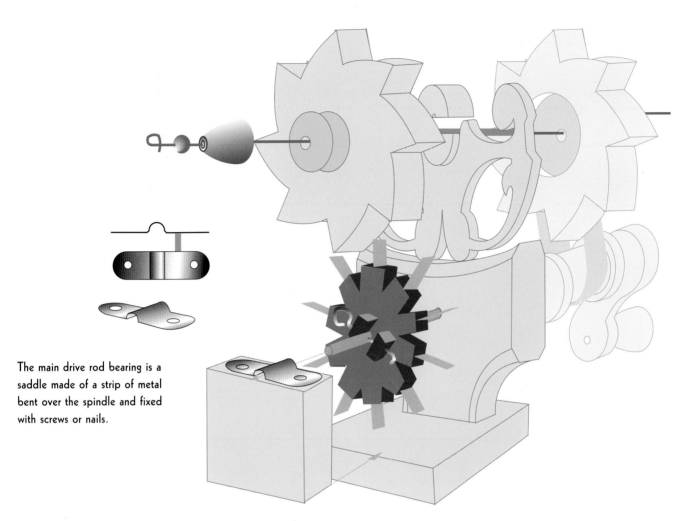

The main drive rod bearing is a saddle made of a strip of metal bent over the spindle and fixed with screws or nails.

Back View

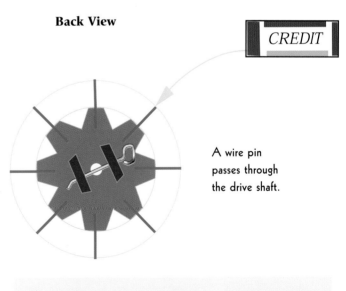

CREDIT

A wire pin passes through the drive shaft.

The rear drive sprocket is armed with bits cut from old credit cards. These slices wear out with use and must be replaced. You will find that some credit cards are better than others. Credit cards are always easy to obtain and are free, if this is all they are used for.

The Best Government . . .

Years ago, when I was a kid of about eight, men used to travel the streets with boxes on sticks. Inside the boxes were little wooden characters that moved. The man wound the handle and miniature workshops—sawing, planing, hammering—sprang to life. This is my version of that wonderful moment when, after giving your penny, the mystery bursts into your mind.

When I heard that a local folk festival wanted buskers, I knew right away what I wanted to make and do. This is it.

They say, "the best government is no government," and that's where I got the title for this piece. What better example of a group working together than a band of musicians. Musicians tell me though that anarchy, despotism, assassinations are pretty much everyday fare for the music biz; so maybe I'm a bit of an idealist, but then I can dream—can't I?

Make of it what I will, the people in this toy are based on real folks. They are a group called "Flapjack." When Jay, the one with the fiddle, saw this he said that here he was immortalized in wood and he wasn't even immortalized in the flesh yet.

Sam, the bass player, got left out of this one but next time—and, this is the great thing about making whacky toys, there is a next time—he'll be there. In fact maybe I could make one of just a bass player. Now I'm thinking that maybe a bass-playing chef (Sam's a chef, too) could lead to some interesting bizzarities!

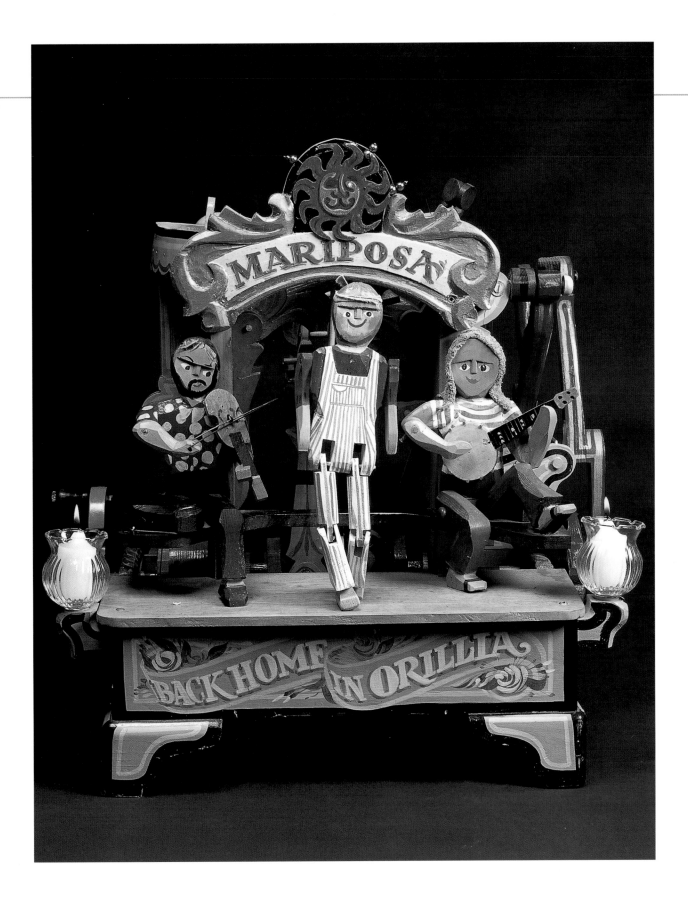

This is the scribble that I sent to the folk festival. This is quite a comprehensive drawing for me. The idea of drawing something out is just to get it set in your mind. To slavishly follow a detailed drawing would be a chore for me and, worse than that, it would close the door on innovation. Later I might use a pencil and paper to work out some detail that my head was having trouble holding.

When you make a little scribble—thoughtfully, mind—of your idea or notion of something that might work, it is amazing how much one puts in that is not visible to anyone but yourself. Maybe this sounds a bit Dutch—if I'm allowed to say that nowadays, 'though my friend Henk, the Netherlander, would say, "No, you're right, that's how we think and talk too!"—but it seems that the putting down of a line if you are thinking of a color will bring that color to mind when you look at it again. It works for me. It'll work for you. Why not?

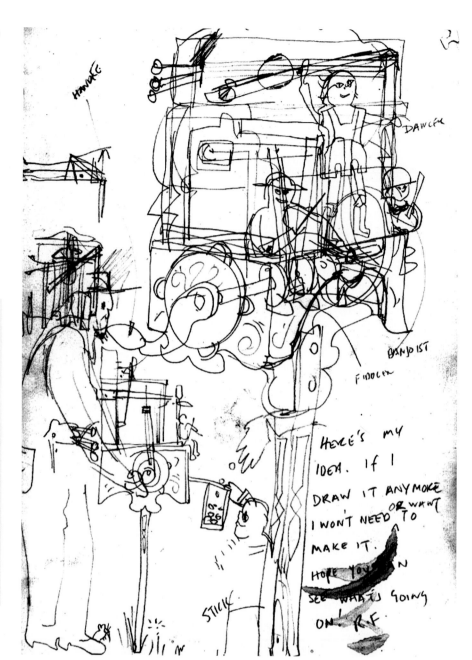

The stick that I was so sure was part of the success of the whole show was a dud. It was awkward and unnecessary and I tripped and fell on it after about five minutes. Lucky I was that I didn't crash down on the whole thing; but, as fate will have it, I seem to have built quite a sturdy piece. After a few minutes limping around, I was on the street again.

I turned the remains of the stick into a stand for Limberjacks and did a pretty good business.

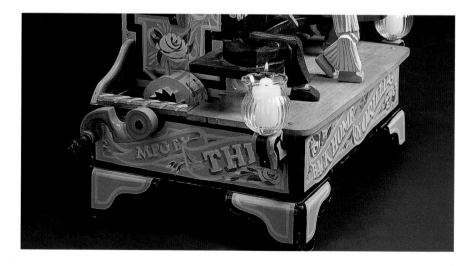

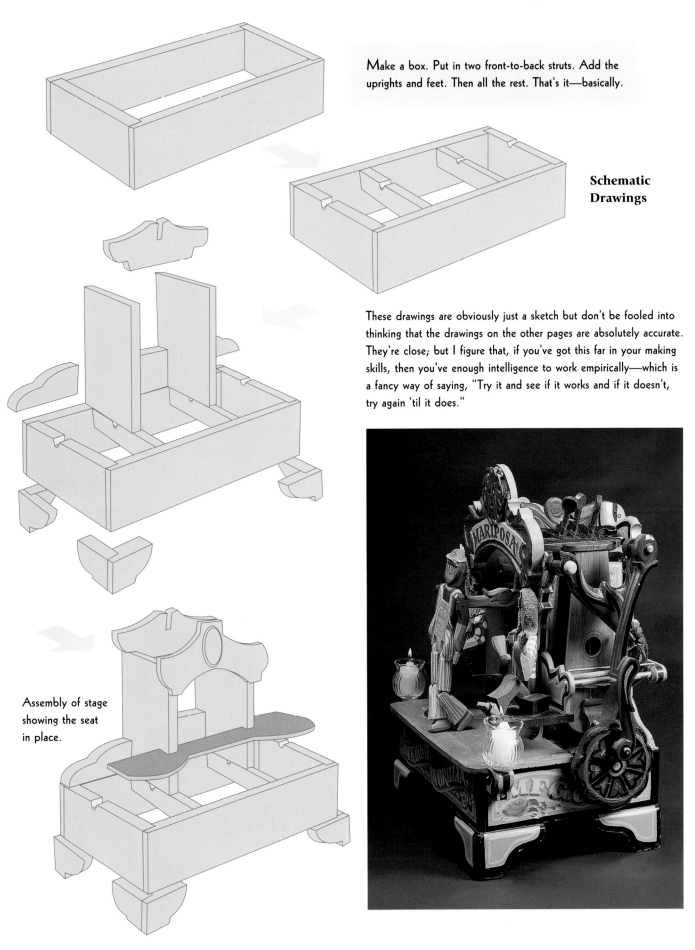

Make a box. Put in two front-to-back struts. Add the uprights and feet. Then all the rest. That's it—basically.

Schematic Drawings

These drawings are obviously just a sketch but don't be fooled into thinking that the drawings on the other pages are absolutely accurate. They're close; but I figure that, if you've got this far in your making skills, then you've enough intelligence to work empirically—which is a fancy way of saying, "Try it and see if it works and if it doesn't, try again 'til it does."

Assembly of stage showing the seat in place.

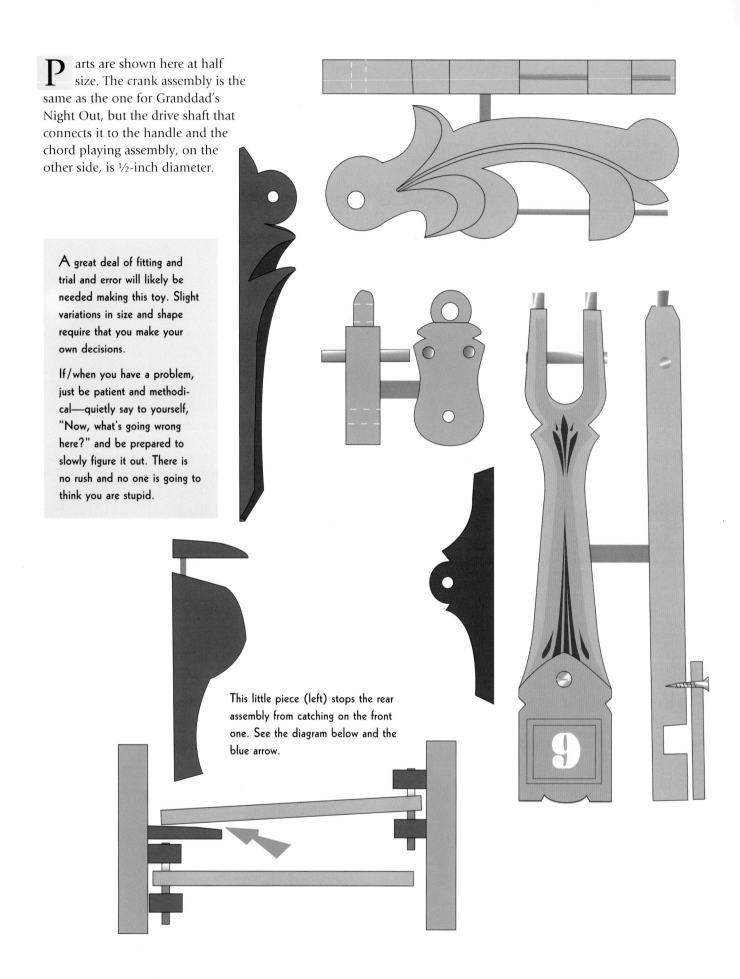

P arts are shown here at half size. The crank assembly is the same as the one for Granddad's Night Out, but the drive shaft that connects it to the handle and the chord playing assembly, on the other side, is ½-inch diameter.

A great deal of fitting and trial and error will likely be needed making this toy. Slight variations in size and shape require that you make your own decisions.

If/when you have a problem, just be patient and methodical—quietly say to yourself, "Now, what's going wrong here?" and be prepared to slowly figure it out. There is no rush and no one is going to think you are stupid.

This little piece (left) stops the rear assembly from catching on the front one. See the diagram below and the blue arrow.

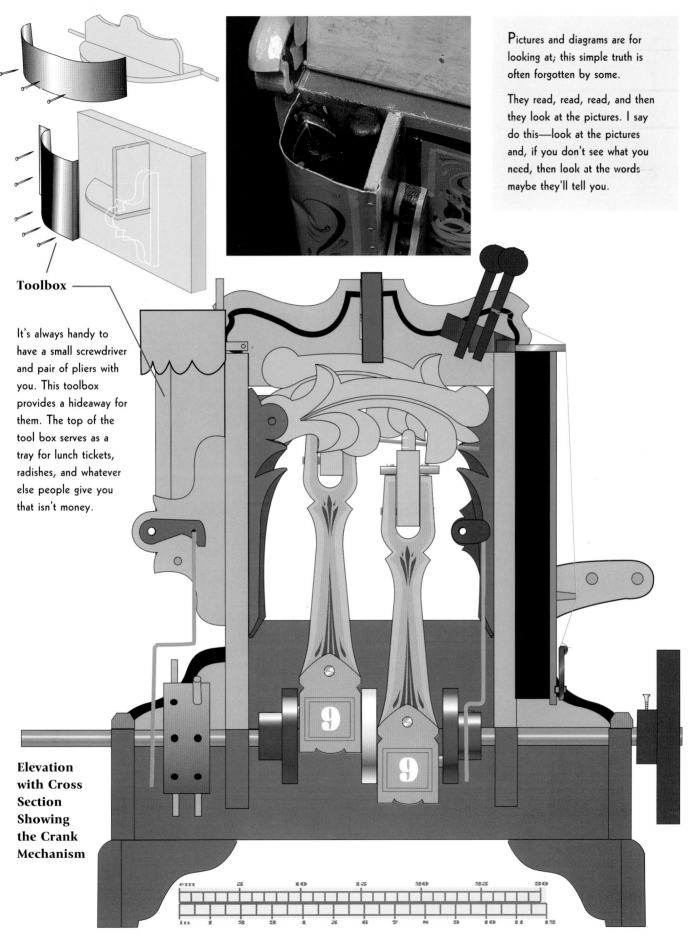

Pictures and diagrams are for looking at; this simple truth is often forgotten by some.

They read, read, read, and then they look at the pictures. I say do this—look at the pictures and, if you don't see what you need, then look at the words maybe they'll tell you.

Toolbox

It's always handy to have a small screwdriver and pair of pliers with you. This toolbox provides a hideaway for them. The top of the tool box serves as a tray for lunch tickets, radishes, and whatever else people give you that isn't money.

**Elevation
with Cross
Section
Showing
the Crank
Mechanism**

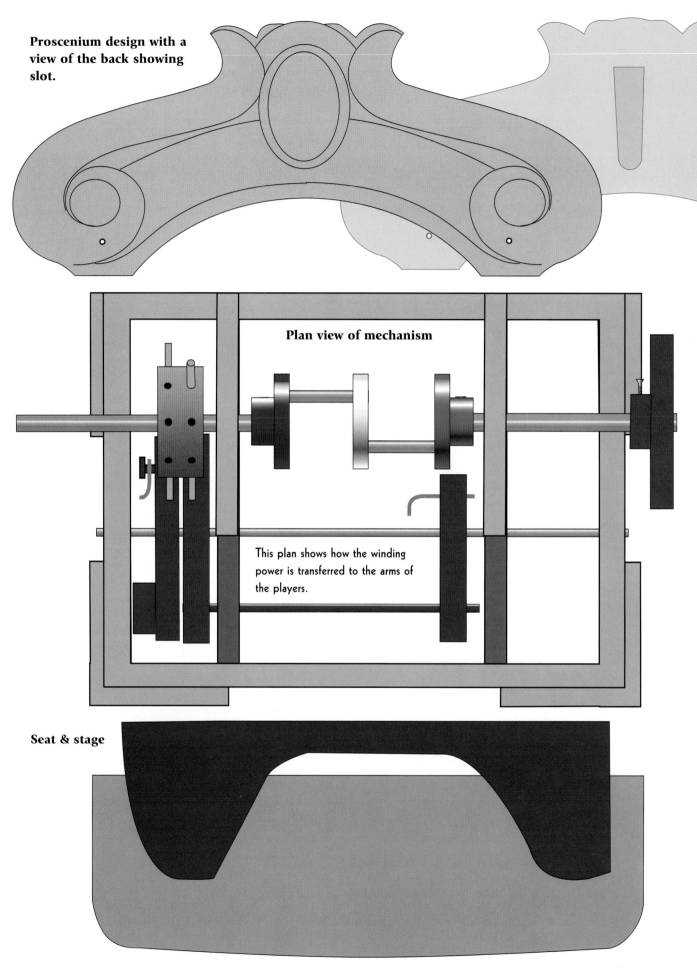

Proscenium design with a view of the back showing slot.

Plan view of mechanism

This plan shows how the winding power is transferred to the arms of the players.

Seat & stage

Detailed patterns for the musicians' legs are not shown since each one is different and determined by the shape of the seat you design.

Carve the instruments to your liking and fit. This is tricky stuff! Look at the photos and figure out how. Difficult, but not impossible.

DETAILS OF THE MECHANISM

How the musicians' arms get to be powered.

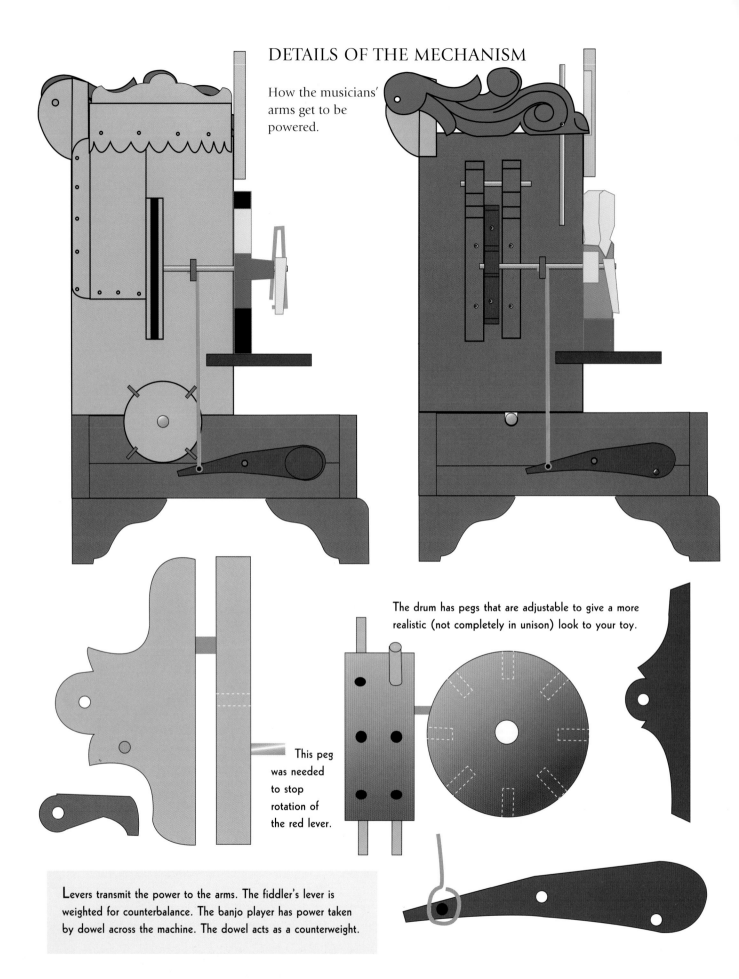

The drum has pegs that are adjustable to give a more realistic (not completely in unison) look to your toy.

This peg was needed to stop rotation of the red lever.

Levers transmit the power to the arms. The fiddler's lever is weighted for counterbalance. The banjo player has power taken by dowel across the machine. The dowel acts as a counterweight.

DANCING ACTION

Why the dancer
jumps up and down.

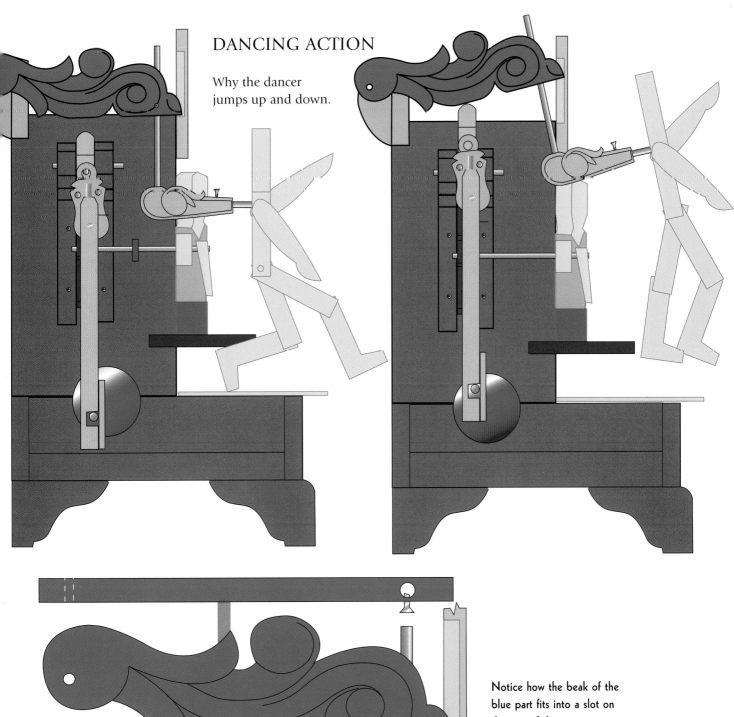

Notice how the beak of the
blue part fits into a slot on
the rear of the proscenium.

Dancer Mechanism

Notice that the front assembly is adjustable
up and down. This is a necessary detail for
getting it to perform well.

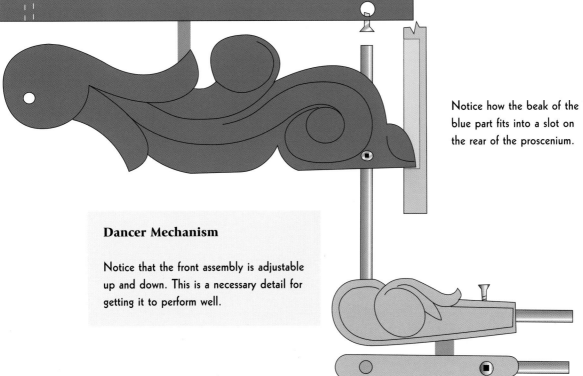

TWANGER ASSEMBLY

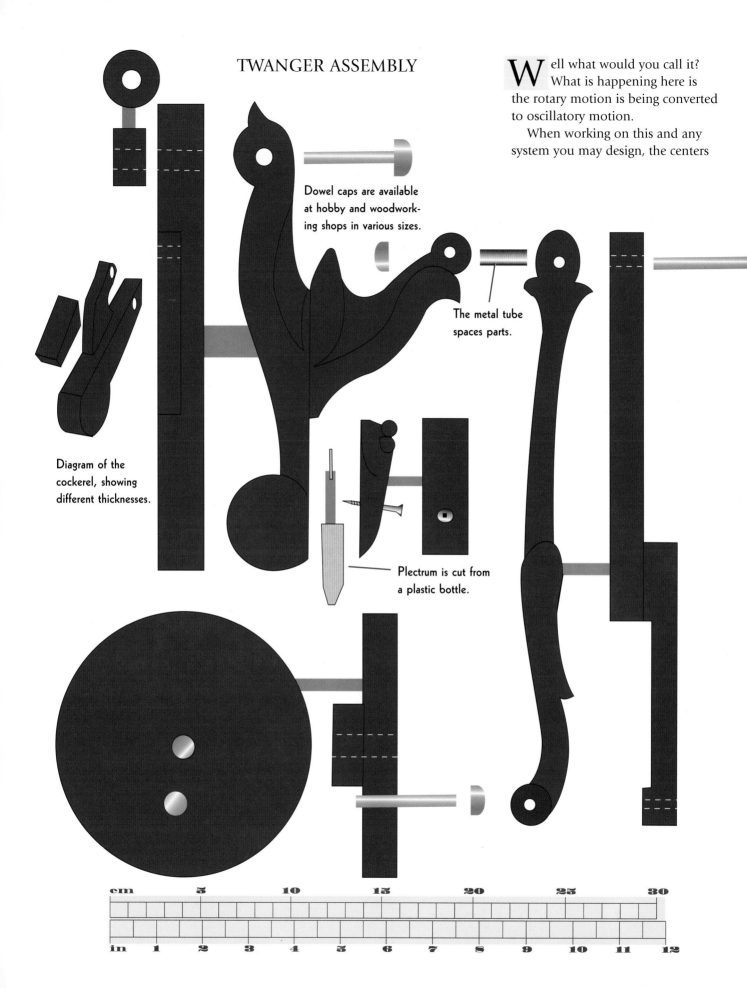

W ell what would you call it? What is happening here is the rotary motion is being converted to oscillatory motion.

When working on this and any system you may design, the centers

Dowel caps are available at hobby and woodworking shops in various sizes.

The metal tube spaces parts.

Diagram of the cockerel, showing different thicknesses.

Plectrum is cut from a plastic bottle.

cm   5   10   15   20   25   30

in   1   2   3   4   5   6   7   8   9   10   11   12

are important. What is between the centers depends on at lot of stuff—cultural and mechanical. Speaking of which, did you ever wonder why some things that are supposedly only based on functional efficiency look different when they come from different people and different countries? For example it's easy to tell an American battleship from a French or British one, yet they all do the same job.

Preferences, ah—preferences!

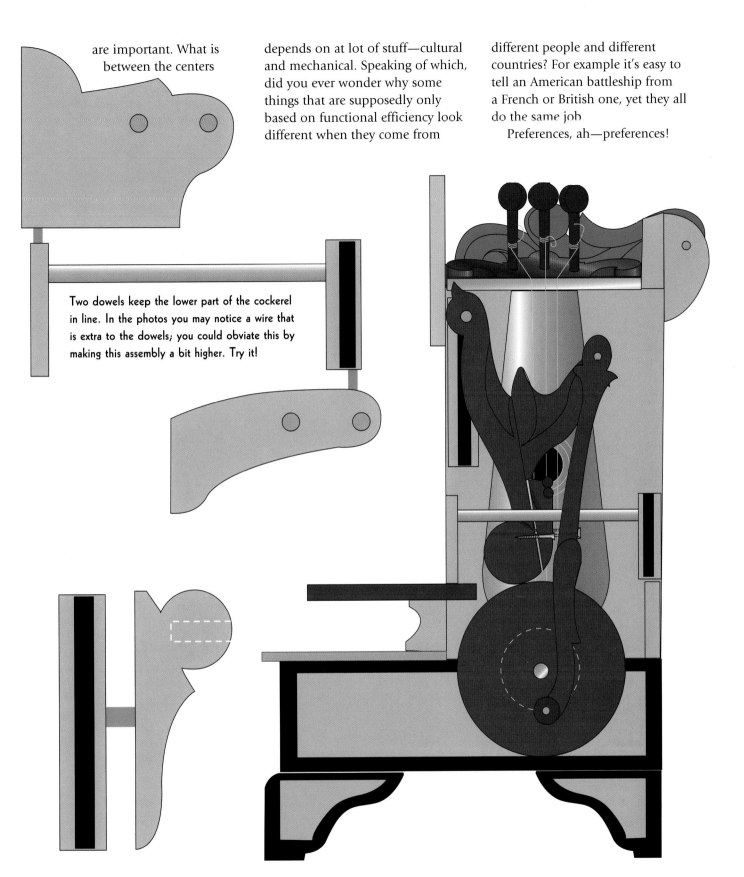

Two dowels keep the lower part of the cockerel in line. In the photos you may notice a wire that is extra to the dowels; you could obviate this by making this assembly a bit higher. Try it!

**Side elevation with cross section showing twanger assembly—
not to the same scale as the parts on this page and opposite**

MONOCHORD

This instrument is, I think, called a monochord, because it plays only one chord. It looks pretty flashy, but it's actually made from the same bits of wood as everything else. When making the pegs and the head piece the pegs fit into, I did treat myself to a bit of mahogany that I had gotten from someone's basement.

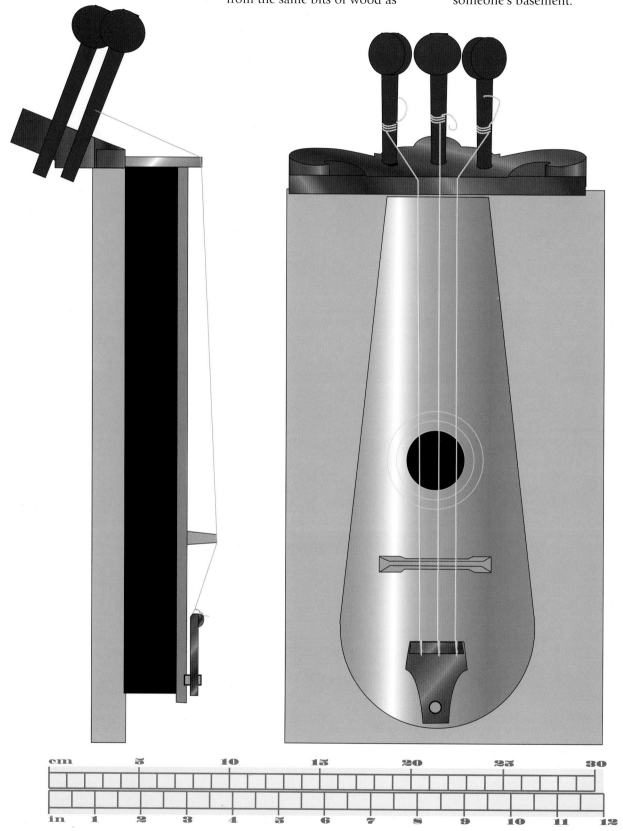

S aw out the rounded lower profile and fit in the sides. What is actually being made here is just a box with round ends. If you think of the essentials, it helps not to get too nervous about making a real musical instrument that sounds out real notes. But having it look nice is part of the fun.

Wood? Pine—what else?? Screw to the backboard.

This is the true shape of the head piece.

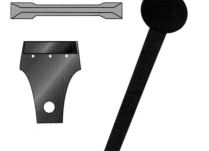

The shape can of course be anything you desire as long as it fits the space available. Be daring—have fun.

The end piece, bridge, and pegs must be hardwood or the steel strings cut right through. Boxwood, lilac, or maple are good.

This bit is called the nut (don't ask why). Make it from some ⅜-inch hardwood—maple is good.

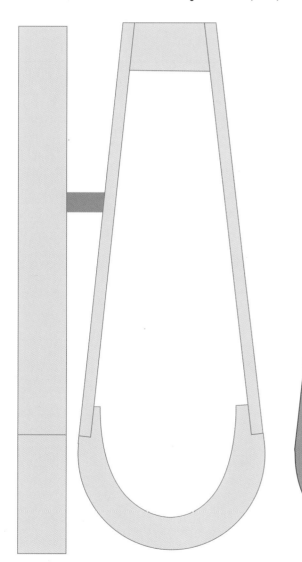

The top is made from ¼-inch pine. Make the box first and then mark its profile on the thin pine top. Cut and shape to look nice. Scribe the decoration before cutting the hole. Glue top to bottom.

Hollow the back as you think fit and for the tone you require. The strings are steel, from a banjo. Steel gives a bright sharp sound; for a more mellow tone (but less carrying) you could use gut or nylon.

Trouble Chuting, a Wild & Wet Whirligig

*S*tarting out is about the hardest thing to get done in any project. After you're started, then the exploring and fun begin. I started this toy as an introduction to a chapter on trouble shooting (a chapter that I have now decided is unnecessary!). Anyhow, I wanted to do a project to illustrate the subject. I didn't want to do anything violent, though, of course, that is what first springs to mind. Maybe because it was the first thing that sprang to mind made me not go there. Well, I'd been racking my feeble enough brain and after a while the French word for white-water rapids surfaced. Chute! It sounds the same as shoot and they are generally trouble. Hard enough to shoot the rapids in a canoe—but in a row boat!? Good luck, little buddy!

Sometimes the most complicated looking things turn out to be the simplest and the easy-looking stuff is really complicated once you get involved with it. Why this is I don't know, but I do know that this little guy in a boat is a pretty tricky project. Be patient and be ready to do something over, when making this toy.

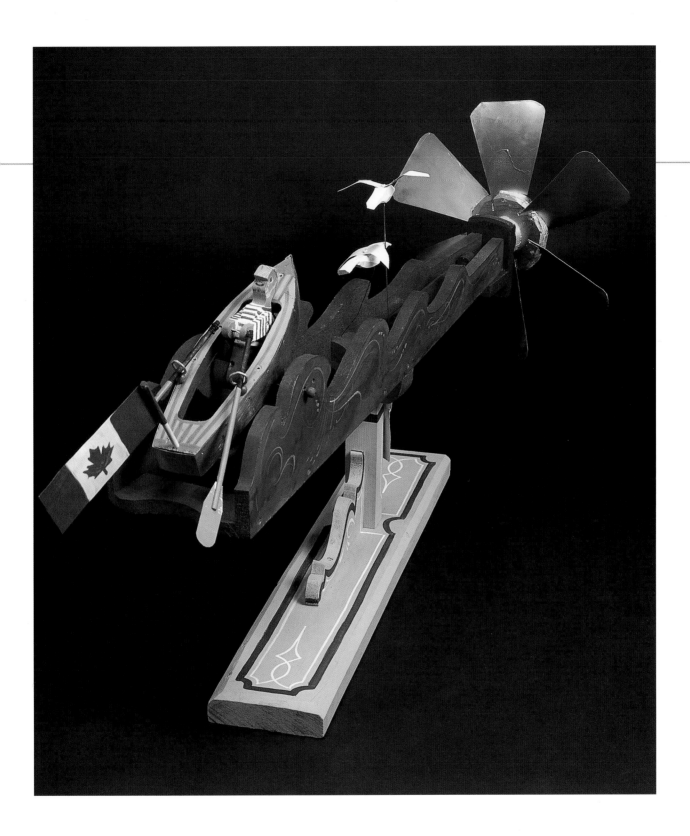

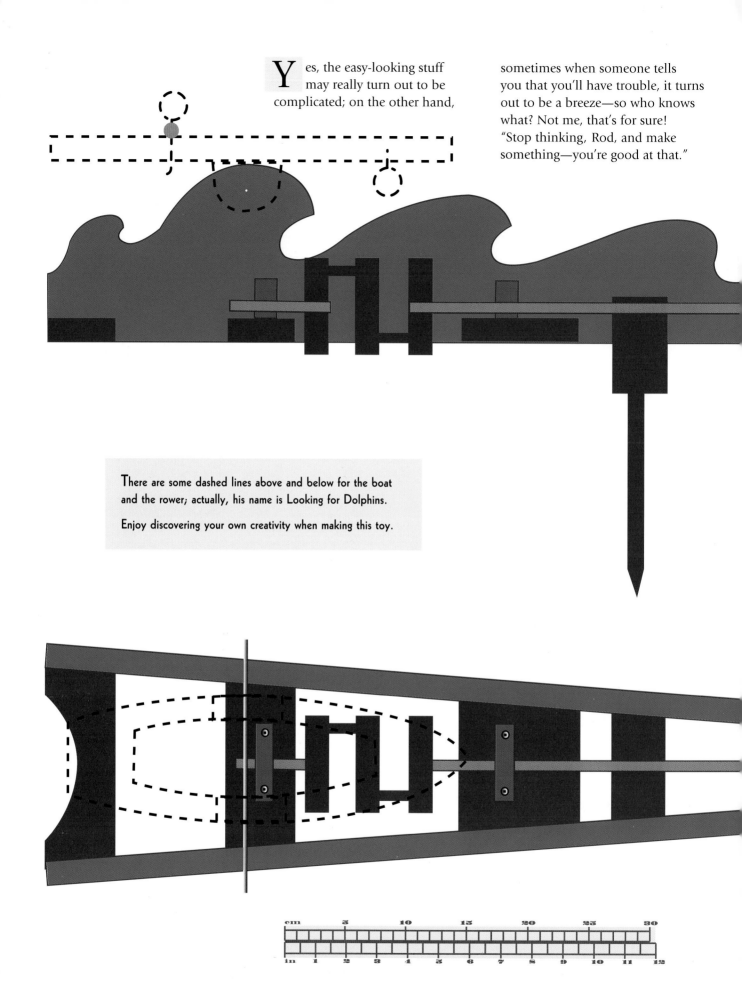

Y es, the easy-looking stuff may really turn out to be complicated; on the other hand, sometimes when someone tells you that you'll have trouble, it turns out to be a breeze—so who knows what? Not me, that's for sure! "Stop thinking, Rod, and make something—you're good at that."

There are some dashed lines above and below for the boat and the rower; actually, his name is Looking for Dolphins.

Enjoy discovering your own creativity when making this toy.

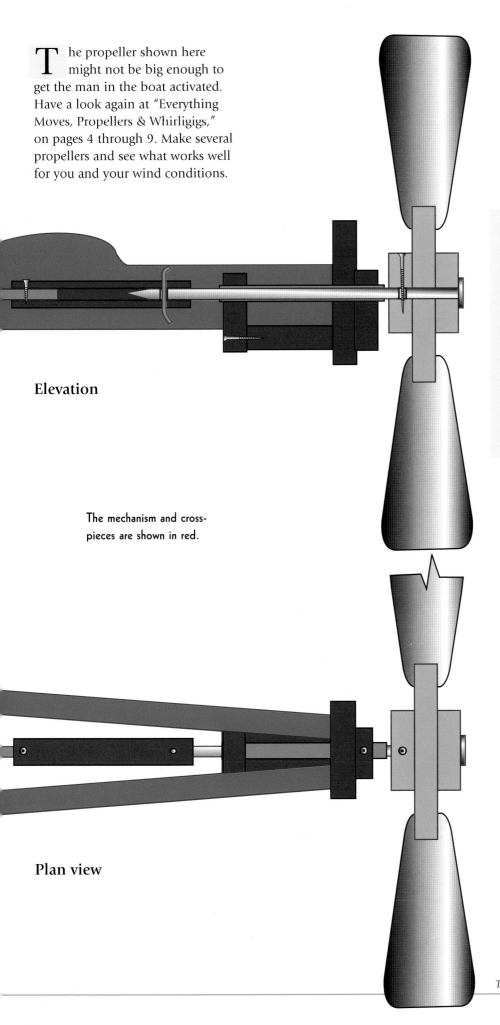

T he propeller shown here might not be big enough to get the man in the boat activated. Have a look again at "Everything Moves, Propellers & Whirligigs," on pages 4 through 9. Make several propellers and see what works well for you and your wind conditions.

The Propeller Assembly

The propeller assembly has a large nail as a spindle. The nail goes through a tube and is joined to the main shaft inside by means of a drilled block. A piece of wire keeps the nail in place.

This arrangement means that you can build and try different propellers quite easily.

Elevation

The mechanism and cross-pieces are shown in red.

Plan view

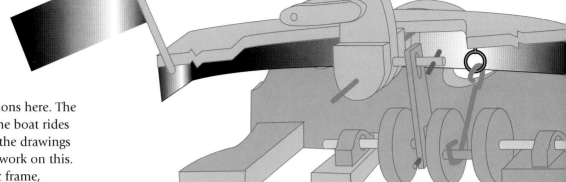

Paint your flag to whatever you want it to be. Make up your own flag!

T here are two actions here. The man rows and the boat rides up and down. Look at the drawings a lot before starting to work on this. After building the basic frame, complete with crank, try the little guy in place without the boat. Adjust the pitman (you might have to make a few before getting it right). When the man is working okay, take him out and work on getting the boat to go up and down.

Now the hard—and possibly frustrating—part; put them both in and get them working together. Next fix in the oars. Sometimes you may have to cut off some of the waves at the back end, since they may interfere with the smooth operation of the oars.

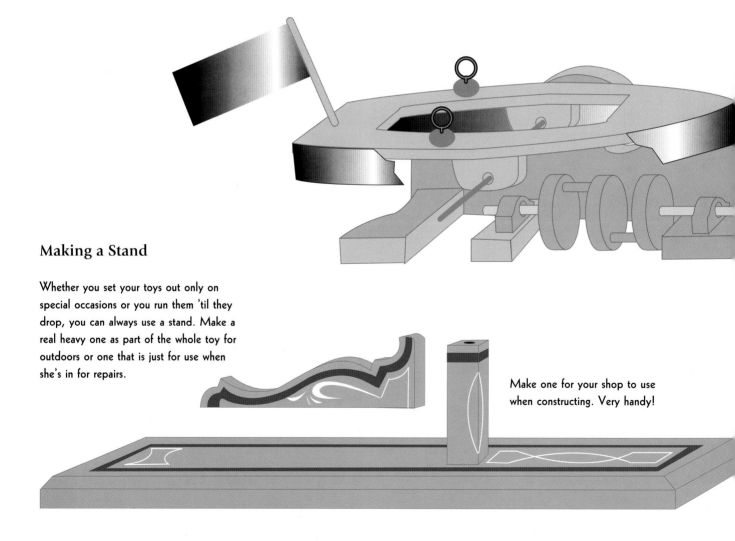

Making a Stand

Whether you set your toys out only on special occasions or you run them 'til they drop, you can always use a stand. Make a real heavy one as part of the whole toy for outdoors or one that is just for use when she's in for repairs.

Make one for your shop to use when constructing. Very handy!

Schematic Drawings of the Mechanism

The propeller can be any shape you wish and need for the conditions in your area. The propeller in the photos may be a bit small; I made it for an indoor exhibition where there wasn't much shelf room.

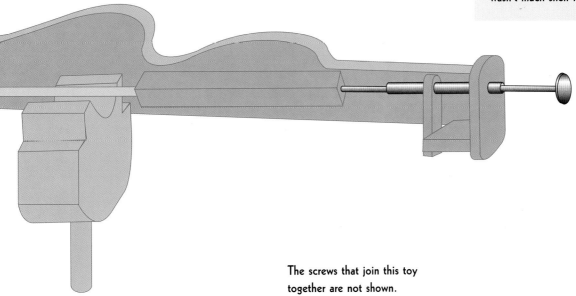

The screws that join this toy together are not shown.

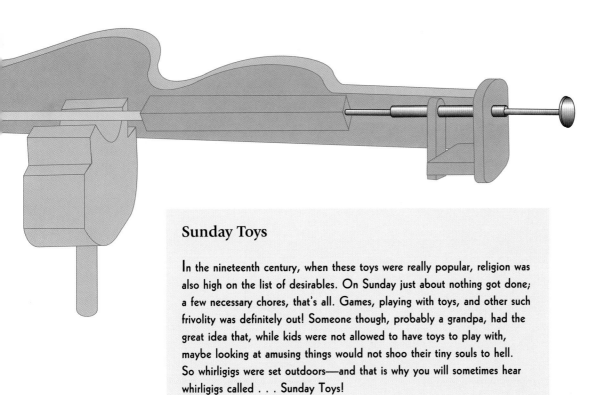

Sunday Toys

In the nineteenth century, when these toys were really popular, religion was also high on the list of desirables. On Sunday just about nothing got done; a few necessary chores, that's all. Games, playing with toys, and other such frivolity was definitely out! Someone though, probably a grandpa, had the great idea that, while kids were not allowed to have toys to play with, maybe looking at amusing things would not shoo their tiny souls to hell. So whirligigs were set outdoors—and that is why you will sometimes hear whirligigs called . . . Sunday Toys!

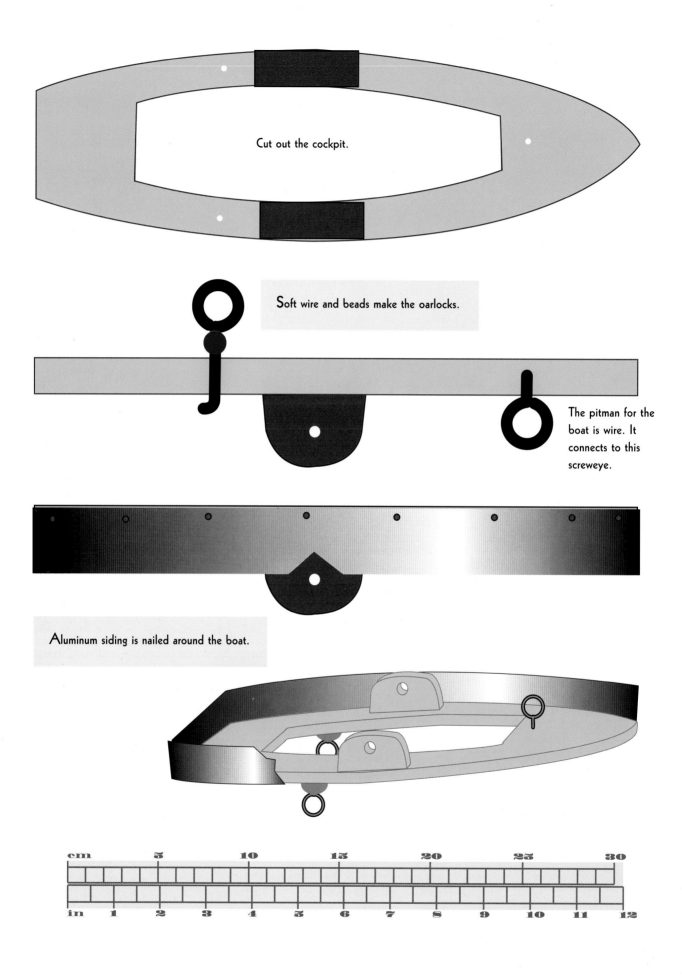

Cut out the cockpit.

Soft wire and beads make the oarlocks.

The pitman for the boat is wire. It connects to this screweye.

Aluminum siding is nailed around the boat.

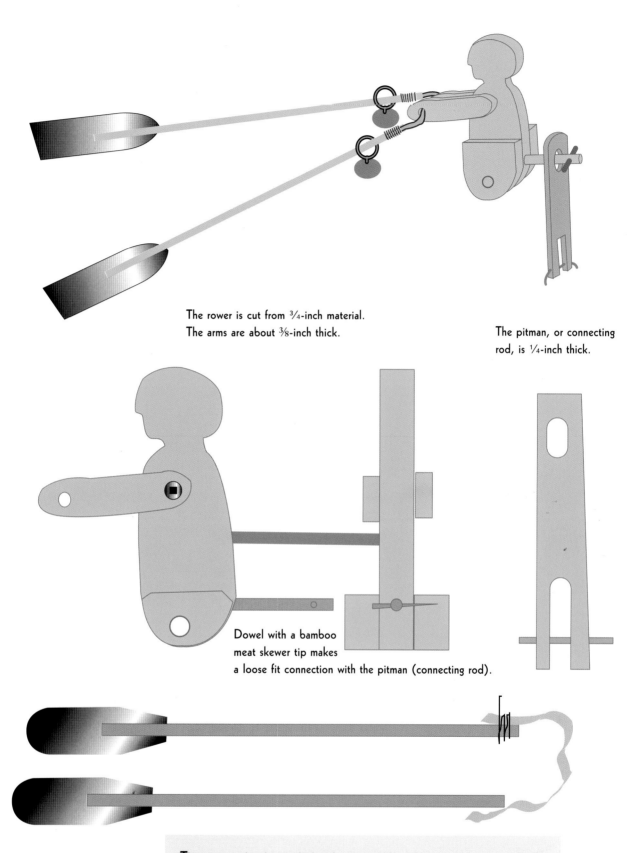

The rower is cut from ¾-inch material.
The arms are about ⅜-inch thick.

The pitman, or connecting
rod, is ¼-inch thick.

Dowel with a bamboo
meat skewer tip makes
a loose fit connection with the pitman (connecting rod).

The oars, made of ¼-inch dowel, are sawn down at one end for the metal oar
blades to be inserted. A strip of thin leather is wired on for a flexible join.
Experiment with the best fit for your toy. Several tries will likely be needed!

The Machine Gunner, a Grisly Whirligig

One of the first toys I ever made was this machine gunner. It was he who decided me on my business name The Grim Reaper Mechanical Toy Company. Here's what happened:

I was sitting in the sun watching a traditional whirligig that I had made, and I started drawing ideas for whirligigs whose subject matter was not your usual cow being milked and so on. I noticed that all the designs I was drawing for possible whirligigs dealt with subjects that had worried and obsessed me during my life of trying to cope with the morbid thoughts that come with clinical depression.

I decided that I would go ahead and make one, turn my terror into a toy—a toy where I was in control. So I made The Machine Gunner and I planned some more. Being involved with them has helped me a lot; I turned my black dogs into pussy cats.

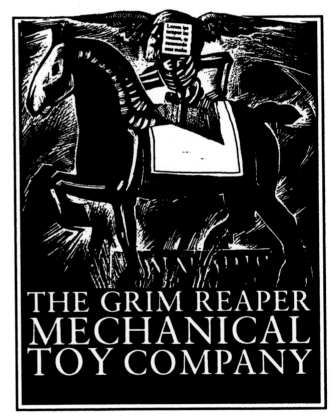

THE GRIM REAPER MECHANICAL TOY COMPANY

The legs are fixed to the
baseboard. The body and
arms are loosely joined so
that they can vibrate with
the movement of the gun.

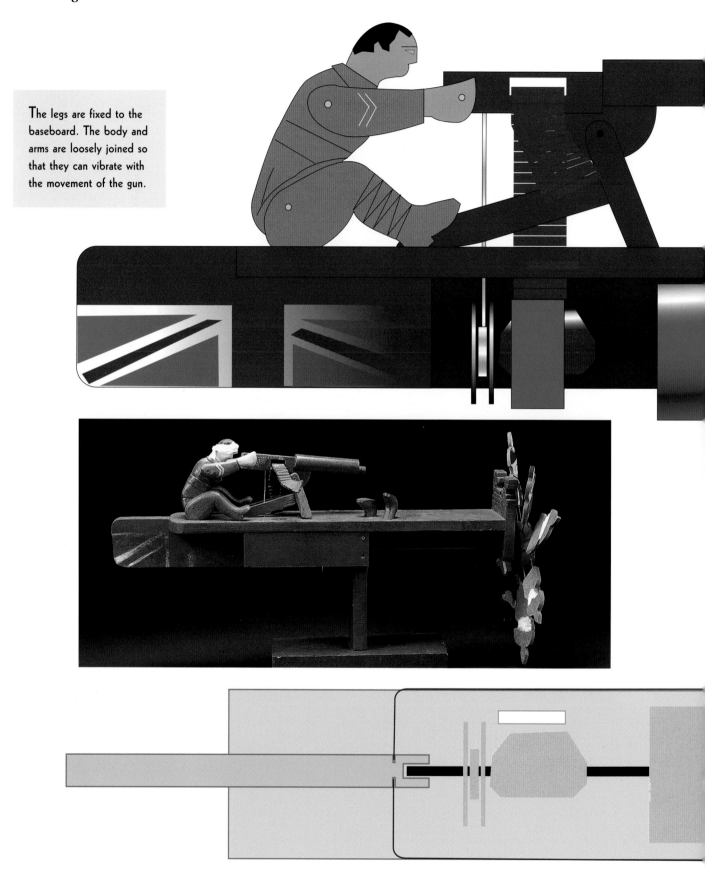

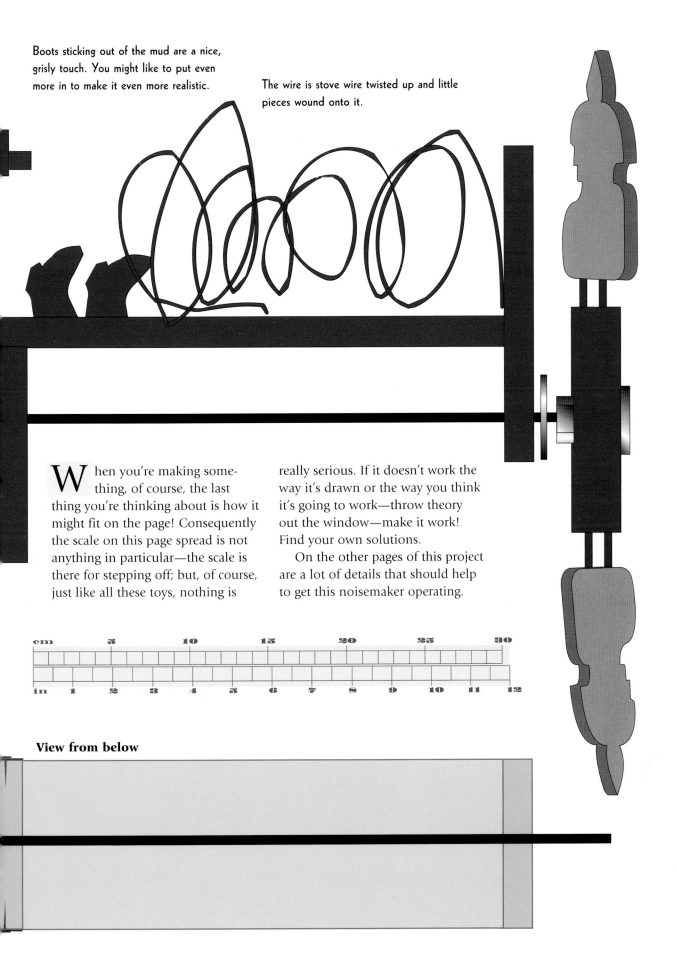

Boots sticking out of the mud are a nice, grisly touch. You might like to put even more in to make it even more realistic.

The wire is stove wire twisted up and little pieces wound onto it.

When you're making something, of course, the last thing you're thinking about is how it might fit on the page! Consequently the scale on this page spread is not anything in particular—the scale is there for stepping off; but, of course, just like all these toys, nothing is really serious. If it doesn't work the way it's drawn or the way you think it's going to work—throw theory out the window—make it work! Find your own solutions.

On the other pages of this project are a lot of details that should help to get this noisemaker operating.

View from below

THE WALL

This wall is really just a sketch; make your own wall however you want it.

When you are designing or modifying whacky toys like these, don't worry about other people. Do your own work. If we took advice from most people, nothing would get done, because everyone has some thing that they don't want to know about.

THE GUNNER

When making the figure of the gunner and fitting it to work, you will find that nothing seems to fit. The pivots are wire pushed through and bent to shape. It takes a great deal of messing around to get it right!

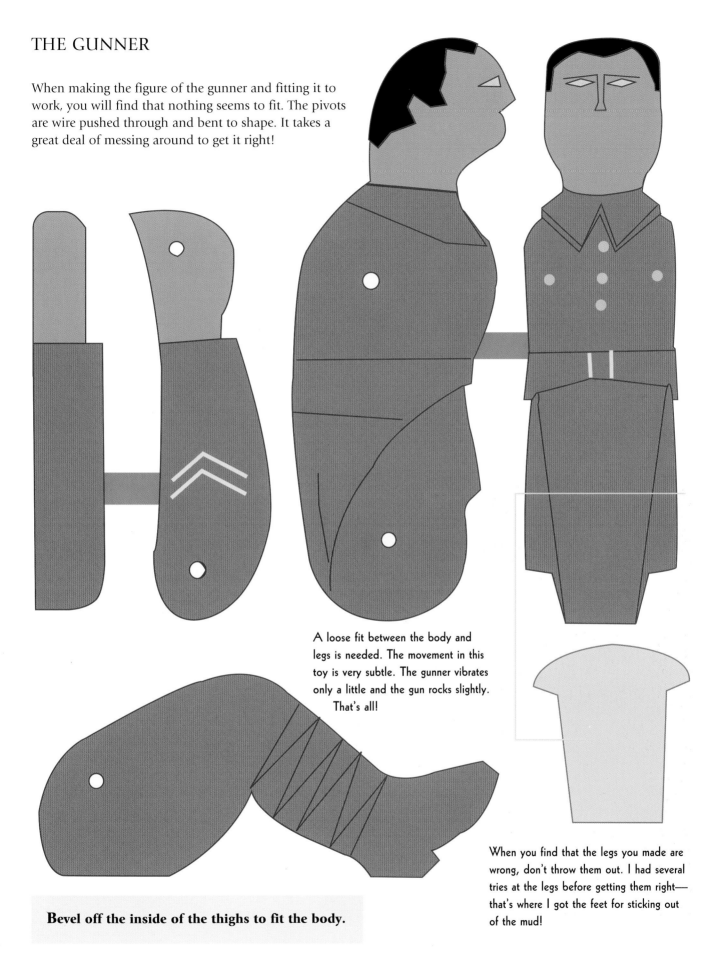

A loose fit between the body and legs is needed. The movement in this toy is very subtle. The gunner vibrates only a little and the gun rocks slightly. That's all!

Bevel off the inside of the thighs to fit the body.

When you find that the legs you made are wrong, don't throw them out. I had several tries at the legs before getting them right—that's where I got the feet for sticking out of the mud!

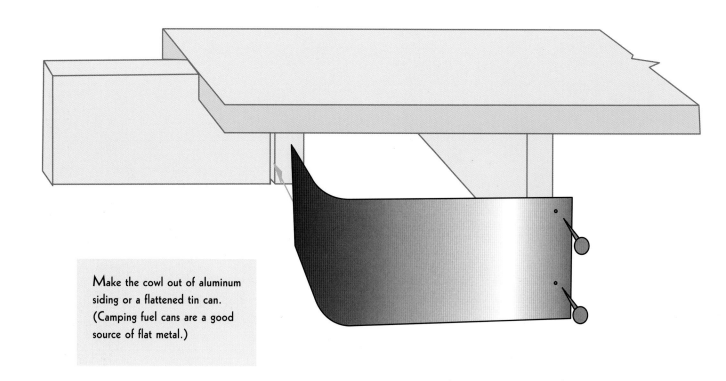

Make the cowl out of aluminum siding or a flattened tin can. (Camping fuel cans are a good source of flat metal.)

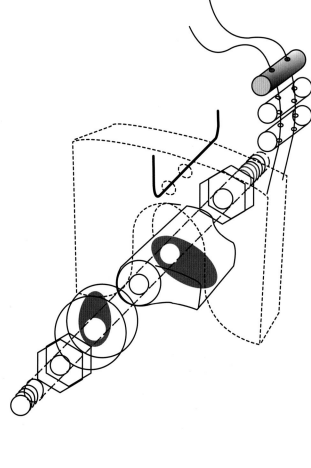

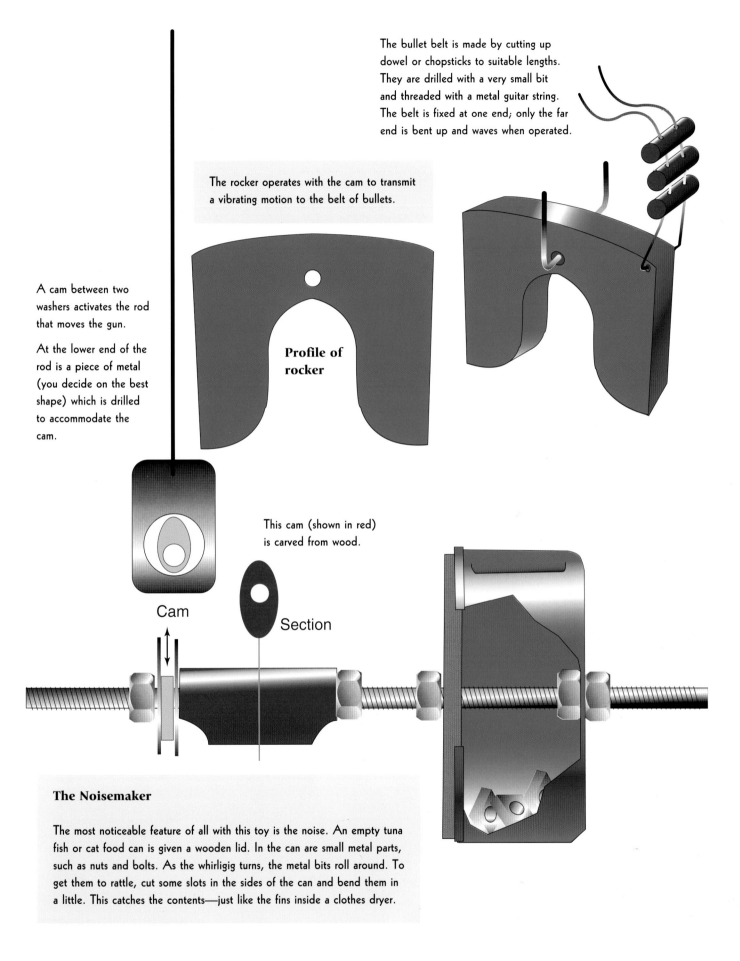

The bullet belt is made by cutting up dowel or chopsticks to suitable lengths. They are drilled with a very small bit and threaded with a metal guitar string. The belt is fixed at one end; only the far end is bent up and waves when operated.

The rocker operates with the cam to transmit a vibrating motion to the belt of bullets.

Profile of rocker

A cam between two washers activates the rod that moves the gun.

At the lower end of the rod is a piece of metal (you decide on the best shape) which is drilled to accommodate the cam.

This cam (shown in red) is carved from wood.

Cam

Section

The Noisemaker

The most noticeable feature of all with this toy is the noise. An empty tuna fish or cat food can is given a wooden lid. In the can are small metal parts, such as nuts and bolts. As the whirligig turns, the metal bits roll around. To get them to rattle, cut some slots in the sides of the can and bend them in a little. This catches the contents—just like the fins inside a clothes dryer.

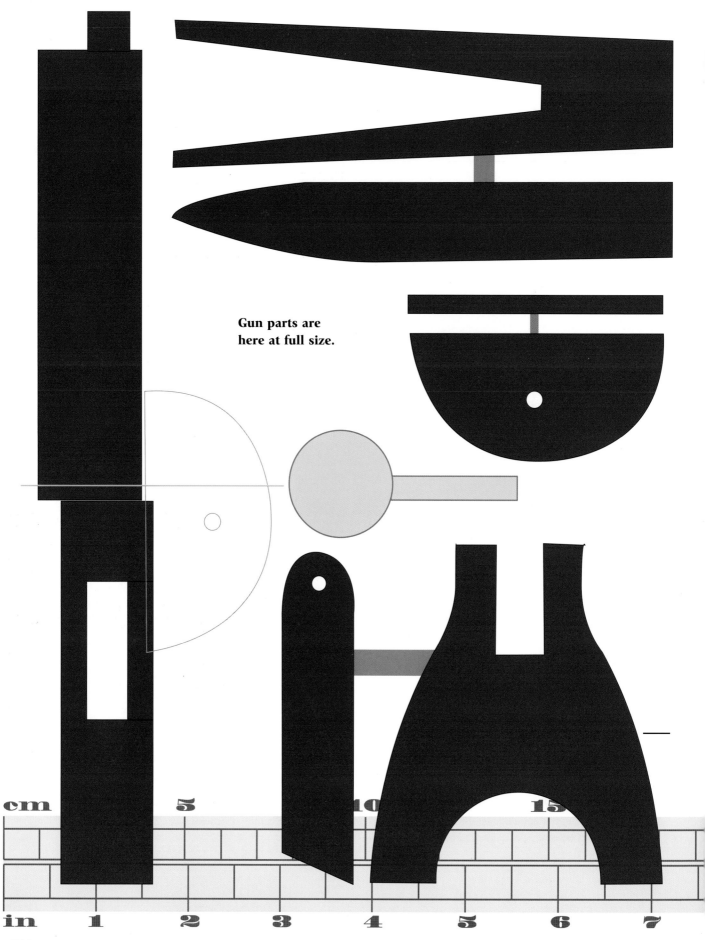

Gun parts are
here at full size.

cm 5 10 15

in 1 2 3 4 5 6 7

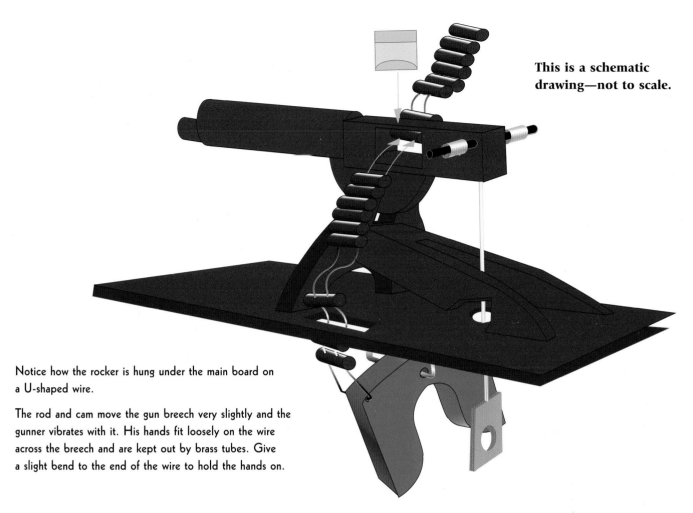

This is a schematic drawing—not to scale.

Notice how the rocker is hung under the main board on a U-shaped wire.

The rod and cam move the gun breech very slightly and the gunner vibrates with it. His hands fit loosely on the wire across the breech and are kept out by brass tubes. Give a slight bend to the end of the wire to hold the hands on.

Use some grease to lubricate the parts. Petroleum jelly (Vaseline) works well and is easy to obtain.

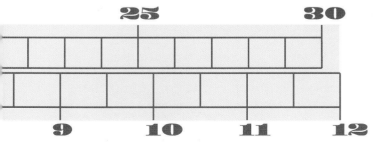

On the outside of this propeller, I have the soldiers in their dress uniforms. On the inside they are wearing field gray.

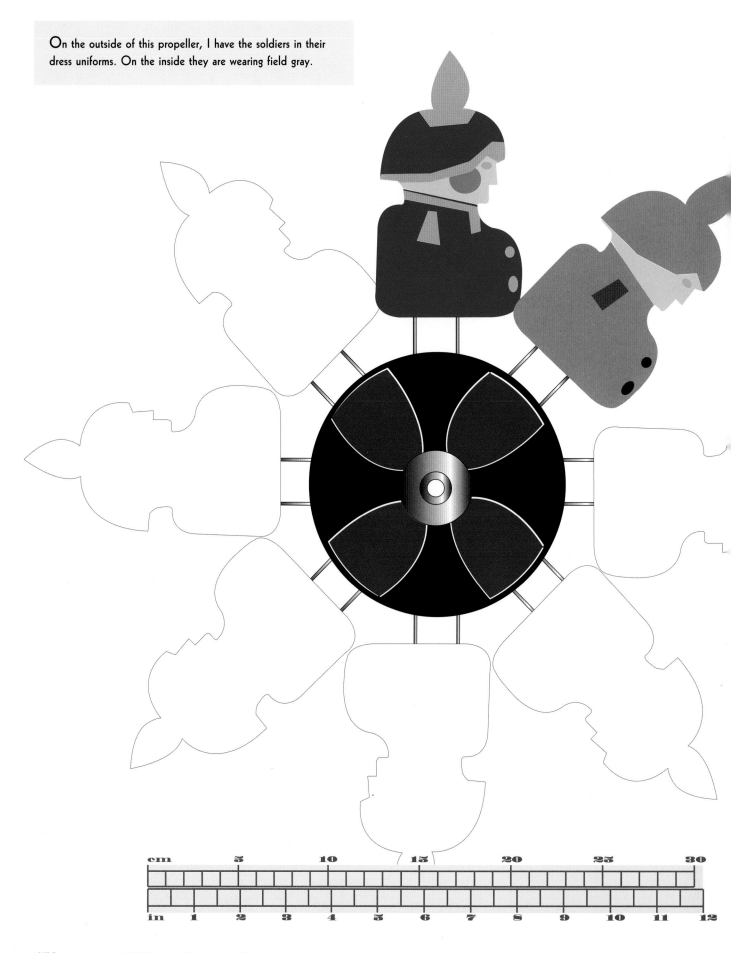

cm 5 10 15 20 25 30

in 1 2 3 4 5 6 7 8 9 10 11 12

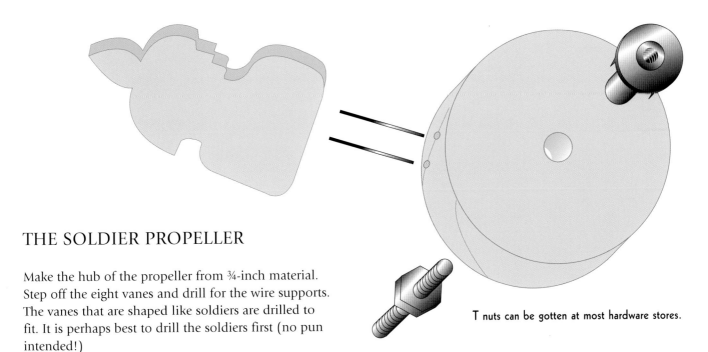

THE SOLDIER PROPELLER

Make the hub of the propeller from ¾-inch material. Step off the eight vanes and drill for the wire supports. The vanes that are shaped like soldiers are drilled to fit. It is perhaps best to drill the soldiers first (no pun intended!)

The center of the hub holds the shaft (threaded rod) on a T nut with a regular nut snugged up to hold it tight.

T nuts can be gotten at most hardware stores.

When making your whirligigs, it is a good idea to consider the direction that your propeller will turn—this can be very frustrating if you have a nut-tightening system for attaching the propeller that the wind will loosen.

Measurement is like a language in that you only need it when you want to communicate with another person or a machine; so don't make a big deal out of it, I say. The drawings in this book may look a lot more precise than they are really meant to be. I don't spend a lot of time worrying about measurements. Try as I might I can never seem to measure something using a ruler and then cut it to fit. Something always seems to go wrong! Yet I can eyeball and cut it to fit right on. The important thing is to check how the piece you're marking is actually going to fit with the others; place it against the place it is intended to fit, to see if it's correct. And then just get on with it!

Metric Equivalents

inches	mm	cm		inches	mm	cm
⅛	3	0.3		12	305	30.5
¼	6	0.6		13	330	33.0
⅜	10	1.0		14	356	35.6
½	13	1.3		15	381	38.1
⅝	16	1.6		16	406	40.6
¾	19	1.9		17	432	43.2
⅞	22	2.2		18	457	45.7
1	25	2.5		19	483	48.3
1¼	32	3.2		20	508	50.8
1½	38	3.8		21	533	53.3
1¾	44	4.4		22	559	55.9
2	51	5.1		23	584	58.4
2½	64	6.4		24	610	61.0
3	76	7.6		25	635	63.5
3½	89	8.9		26	660	66.0
4	102	10.2				
4½	114	11.4				
5	127	12.7		inches	feet	m
6	152	15.2				
7	178	17.8		12	1	0.305
8	203	20.3		24	2	0.610
9	229	22.9		36	3	0.914
10	254	25.4		48	4	1.219
11	279	27.9		60	5	1.524

Conversion Factors

mm	=	millimeter		m	=	meter
cm	=	centimeter		m^2	=	square meter
1 mm	=	0.039 inch		1 inch	=	25.4 mm
1 m	=	3.28 feet		1 foot	=	304.8 mm
1 m^2	=	10.8 square feet		1 sq ft	=	0.09 m^2

Index

Any writer can be made into this toy. He doesn't actually write, but his arm moves back and forth clicking and his head kind of follows the writing. The photograph above and the drawing to the right give you some hints of how you might create the mechanism for this popular toy. A crank, a sprocket, a bit of spring wire, some pegs, and you're set to devise the movement. Try it!

Arm   Head